The Volunteer Library

THE VOLUNTEER LIBRARY

A Handbook

by

LINDA S. FOX

McFarland & Company, Inc., Publishers
Jefferson, North Carolina, and London

Library of Congress Cataloguing-in-Publication Data

Fox, Linda S., 1944–
The volunteer library : a handbook / by Linda S. Fox
p. cm.
Includes bibliographical references and index.
ISBN 0-7864-0679-8 (sewn softcover : 50# alkaline paper) ∞
1. Volunteer libraries—United States.   2. Association libraries—
United States.   3. Rural libraries—United States.   I. Title.
Z675.V84F69   1999   025—dc21
99-29847 CIP

British Library Cataloguing-in-Publication data are available

Manufactured in the United States of America

McFarland & Company, Inc., Publishers
Box 611, Jefferson, North Carolina 28640

www.mcfarlandpub.com

To the volunteers of Capitan Public Library:
without your determination and dedication
there would be no library in Capitan, New Mexico, today.

And to my husband, Hugh,
who keeps me going strong.

Acknowledgments

To the following people who have given me inspiration, opportunity, guidance and support I offer my thanks and my affection:

Debbie Coover, Nancy Rubery, Linda Benedict, Cynthia Lopata, Laura Dickey, Pam Johnson, John LaRock, Barbara Settel, Ruth Small, Sam Oh, Patty Fletcher and Monica Bock.

Ours is a special and rewarding comradeship. It is my hope that this book will help and inspire others to join us.

Table of Contents

Preface

The careful creation of a small library in a rural, remote community can fill educational, cultural and recreational needs; doors can be opened to knowledge and dreams, and a new kind of community service can be experienced. I have seen this happen. Even with our amazing information technology, throughout the creation process there still stand the non-technical library necessities of planning, managing and inspiration.

A library is a natural outgrowth of one or multiple emotions:

- A deep love of reading and of books
- The yen to organize materials and make them somehow accessible
- The nudge of curiosity and the continuing drive to learn
- Childhood memories of a safe and dependable library environment
- A desire to serve and enrich one's community.

In a community without a library, such comments and questions as these may be heard:

- Why don't we have a library?
- I wish I could take my kids to the library.
- The closest library is so far away!
- The bookmobile is great, but we need something more.

And the big question: Why can't we start our own library right here?

Since you are sitting there holding this book in your hand, I assume some or all of the above is familiar! And the response to the big question—Why can't we start a library?—is a resounding, "You can!"

If your group is not in the enviable position of having money available to you through an interested and benevolent donor, or if your community cannot bond for library money and thus hire a professional director, this book is for you.

I have two reasons for writing this handbook: (1) a dedication to the small rural public library, its role in the community, and to helping people like you; (2) an understanding of your desire to create the best possible library.

I strongly believe (because I have seen) that if a dedicated and cooperative group of people is given basic explanations, guidelines, lists, samples and directions to further information (along with pep talks), it can succeed in creating a real library.

You will want to find out what the job entails: Figures representing the fictional towns of Baird and Handleberg in "Your State" are presented to help show the process of a library creation. Practical worksheets from Appendix B can be used as you plan your library.

I also understand your desire to do the best job possible. After working within the library environment for fifteen years, I went back to school (at the age of fifty) to earn a master of library science degree to improve my own performance and understanding of librarianship. I have been involved with groups like yours (with very little or no money) in rural areas of several states (Vermont, upstate New York and New Mexico).

Having said all that, I need to add that it is hard work. I can give you explanations, but there my role ends—yours will be just starting. If, having read the handbook, you decide to go on and create your community's library—good luck, and let me know when you open the doors!

— Part One —
Required Reading

1

Commitments
and the Core Group

For a volunteer library to succeed, the group behind it must meet three criteria absolutely:

- Commitment of interest
- Commitment of time
- Seed money from within the group

These criteria must be met by what I call the "core group." This will be the initial decision-making group. When this group has met its mission and laid the groundwork, it may be replaced by or become the library board of trustees. Core group members will attend all meetings, gather information, represent the library project and read all communications. In short, group members are those who "know what's going on."

Obviously this kind of commitment cannot be the on-again off-again kind of commitment. Perhaps you are reading this book because you personally have made a commitment and are wondering where to go next. You may have a core group in mind, and just want advice on how to approach them for the job. Whichever the situation, there is plenty of helpful information.

First I want to talk about three criteria—interest, time and seed money—and why the core group should meet them. Chapter 2 is devoted to the actual formation of the core group.

Interest

It goes without saying that many people will be interested in wanting to start a library. It is a good idea to ask exactly what that interest is in order to find out how deep it goes. Do not assume everyone's interest will be the same.

Someone may just want to circulate books, while another might like to have a study hall for students, and someone else may want to provide a place to sit and read a free newspaper every week. Occasionally parents may want to have a place to "bring the kids" when they go shopping, while some people could need homeschooling materials. A person might want to be involved in the clerical side of things, while someone else wants to decorate the place. People may view the library as a likely social gathering site for the community, and still others may consider it a "quiet zone" at all times for peaceful study and thought.

And of course there will be people who have a sincere interest in setting up a library in the traditional sense; a library where information and recreational reading materials can be organized, retrieved and used.

At an initial meeting of everyone in the community interested in starting a library, time should be allowed for people to express these seemingly disparate ideas and a record should be kept. Such a record (Interests/Expectations of Supporters' Group) is valuable because it reveals the community's personality and desires, as we will see when we later discuss assessing the Community.

Figure 1.1 presents a sample record of varying interests.

(See Worksheet 1.1, Appendix B.)

Time

Starting a library sounds easy: just get some books donated, get a desk and some shelves, and let 'em flow in and out the door, right? If you are only interested in a second-hand lending library, you may be right in that vision. But if you are after something more—a library which organizes, circulates and makes accessible pleasure reading and information—then your level of interest must extend to actual hard work.

The commitment of time is essential; the fewer other commitments, the better. There are not a lot of people who are going to have the necessary time. Such a demand will separate the supporters from the core group.

A word of caution as you develop the core group: Don't minimize the time and work involved. To say "It will take a definite commitment of time and work" is better than "Oh, it should just be some meetings and if you can't get to them all, that'll be okay—we know you have a lot to do." This last state-

---

Figure 1.1
Sample of Citizen Interest and
Experience Table

Interest/ Expectation	*Name*	*Note/ Experience*	*Phone, etc.*
Preschool storytime	Sally Jenkins	Has puppet theater	777-3407
Place to type papers	Bill Smith	HS student; can clean	777-6565
Chance to see folks	Joe Harnett	Could work at desk; can alphabetize	777-5454

---

ment undermines the seriousness of what you are undertaking and will waste time at meetings; someone will always need to be given an overview of previous discussions.

Here is a suggestion: prepare a Statement of Commitment. When the group presents the project to others, this statement will demonstrate their seriousness and dedication. Figure 1.2 provides an example.

Think of such a commitment as needing a defined period of time with specific chores to be done, after which satisfaction can be enjoyed by all!

(See Worksheet 1.2, Appendix B.)

Seed Money from Within the Group

This is a difficult area to some people, but I feel it is a commitment as equally necessary as interest and time. Seed money starts a project; for it to originate within the group speaks loudly and clearly about the seriousness of their library project. After all, they will be going forth to ask others for financial support!

I am not talking about thousands of dollars at this point. I am suggesting that once the core group is assembled, they give what they can toward the library's beginning. This can be either an outright contribution or a pledge. For some that may be a lump sum of $100 to $200, to another it will be $30, and there may be someone who can indeed give $1,000 or more. Another may opt to pledge a set amount every month rather than a lump sum. This demonstrates a faith that the project will become permanent.

Some members of the core group may ask to remain anonymous in their pledge or contribution to the project; however, anonymity is not recommended. After all, the point of such a contribution is to demonstrate serious intent and

---

Figure 1.2
Sample Statement of Commitment

STATEMENT OF COMMITMENT OF THE HANDLEBERG LIBRARY COMMITTEE

We, the undersigned, do hereby pledge ourselves to the task of creating a library for Handleberg. In doing so, we commit to the project by:

• Attending all bimonthly meetings
• Meeting with consultants if meetings cannot be scheduled at bimonthly meetings
• Maintaining individual notebooks with all relevant paperwork
• Being responsible for one major area of concern toward the library's development
• Learning as much about the running and welfare of libraries as we can
• Contributing a monetary amount towards the project

We understand that we are part of a group and cannot make decisions on behalf of the core group without proper discussion beforehand. We will keep core group business confidential.

Signed: Date:

1.
2.
3.
4.
5.

---

dedication to the task ahead. As other supporters and funders see these members have "put their money where their mouths are," they will be encouraged to add their own donations.

CREATE A RECORD OF THE NEW FUND

A special record of this initial commitment should be created A sample record is shown in Figure 1.3.

Esther, you notice, waited to see how serious everyone else was before she made her generous contribution. This can happen; it is human nature. Remember, everyone should contribute if a statement of commitment was signed. People may need to be reminded they committed to contribute or pledge; that is also human nature.

(See Worksheet 1.3, Appendix B.)

**Figure 1.3
Sample of Initial Financial Donations
by Core Group Members**

The Handleberg Library Committee has individually pledged or contributed to the Library Project Fund. This money will provide the "Seed Money" needed for basic supplies particular to the project, possible travel expenses for consultants, pertinent reference books, and any start-up costs we may encounter. In this way, we demonstrate our faith in the project and our determination to do the best work possible. An accounting of all costs and expenditures will be kept.

Contributor	*Amount*	*Date*
Sarah Guest	$125.00	January 4, 1999
William Wilder	$35.00	January 4, 1999
Genny Folks	$100.00 (quarterly)	January 18, 1999
Chris Whitel	$50.00	January 18, 1999
Benny Jenx	$20.00 (monthly)	January 25, 1999
Suellen Lamour	$5.00 (monthly)	January 31, 1999
Esther Schwinn	$1500.00	February 7, 1999

CREATE A BANK ACCOUNT

Give the newly established fund a name. Open a bank account and have checks printed in the name of the fund. Keep a careful accounting of its use; it is damaging to any project not to be able to explain where money goes. Others will be encouraged to give to the fund, and a good accounting is comforting as well as legally important.

WHAT ABOUT IN-KIND CONTRIBUTIONS?

In-kind contributions are services and or items offered in lieu of money. In-kind donations would be better coming from the supporters group; the core group can give both kinds of donations, but should definitely give money. Keep a list of suggested in-kind contributions; this is invaluable information for the core group when needs arise. Because many of the library project supporters may have in-kind services to offer, they should be included on this list.

Figure 1.4 presents an example of these in-kind services.

(See Worksheet 1.4, Appendix B.)

Figure 1.4
Potential In-Kind Services

FOR THE HANDLEBERG LIBRARY PROJECT
GENERAL LIBRARY MEETING
FEBRUARY 1, 1999

1. Chris Whitel	adding machine & tapes	777-7890
2. Mike Current	two folding tables and five folding chairs	777-5555
3. Williams' Market	free use of copy machine	see Ellen
4. Handleberg News	space for library news	777-5643
5. Esther Schwinn	desk, file cabinet	777-2002
6. Benny Jenx	accounting experience	777-5454

2

Roles Within the Core Group

How Many Roles Are There?

In addition to the interest, time and seed money criteria for a core group, there are further things to consider when forming the group.

First of all there are the various jobs to be done while the group meets and works together. The positions—or roles—which I think are key to the group are:

- Chairman—he or she knows the schedule and is authorized to make decisions "on the spot"; calls meetings and presides at them
- Treasurer
- Recording Secretary—also takes care of communications
- Someone with legal knowledge
- Contact person at the state, county or system library level (see Chapter 26).

Represent the Community!

If you read down the list and said, "Oh, I can come up with people who can do that. We're all set," don't be too sure! Beside just the jobs those positions suggest, I want to impress on you that the core group needs to be representative of all segments of the community; they should represent your community's character.

Even though you haven't yet done a full community profile (assessment), you already know a lot about the character of your community; you can and should have all these characteristics represented in the core group. This makes sense for several reasons, all of which have merit:

- It will truly represent all facets of the community.
- You will not be accused (or suspected) of being a cozy little group.
- The project will benefit from a variety of backgrounds and expertise.
- A sample of community needs will be brought out as you proceed together.

Doesn't that make good sense? Otherwise, if only a few like-minded people worked on a library project, some needs, possibilities, local issues and demographic considerations could easily be overlooked and not included in the planning (see Chapter 7).

Keeping all these things in mind, begin to assemble the core group for your library much as you would assemble the ingredients for a good meal in your home: You bring together the vegetables, rolls or bread, potato or rice or pasta, type of salad, meat (or vegetarian alternative) and dessert that will allow guests to enjoy the kind of meal they all enjoy. It will be seasoned to their tastes and you will consider this as you mix ingredients together.

Just as your meal will be particular to your guests, your library should be particular to your community. This is also how you decide what the library's role in the community will be—bon appétit!

COMMUNITY CHARACTERISTICS

Try describing the makeup of your community (the guests who will be eating that meal) by jotting down and discussing the following community segments or, as I prefer to use, community characteristics.

- Age Range—

  Consider younger and older elements. Is there noticeably more of one than the other? Is there a Head Start? A Senior Center?
- Cultural Diversity—

  Be careful not to assume there is none; consider seasonal workers, native populations and recent arrivals from other countries.
- Old-timers and Newcomers—

  Both groups are important. Their concerns and suggestions are valuable.

- Educational Establishments—

  How many, and is there close involvement between them and the community? Is there a homeschool network?

- Business—

  Are there a lot, or a only a few businesses in town? Do they draw people from other areas? Is there a chamber of commerce? How do they promote the community?

- Service, Social Groups and Religious Organizations—

  American Legion, Boy Scouts, quilters, garden clubs, Jaycees, Rotary, Elks, Lions, PTO or PTA, sports teams, church and synagogue groups. Think: what do people join?

- Arts and Cultural Environment—

  Artists, writers, theater groups, music clubs, book clubs, museums, sports areas.

  Are there a lot of people involved in these areas?

- Local Government—

  Those "in the know" and who have the "power."

Any I might have missed? Remember, these are the characteristics (segments) that make it your unique community.

If the Shoe Fits

Ready for the next big step? Go ahead and ask yourselves: Who comes to mind when we talk about these segments of our community? Who would have both beneficial insight into these segments and be valuable to the core group in one of its roles?

Remember, you already have a list showing who has the time, interest and seed money (optional). Now consider them in this new light of community representation.

Since the library board officers may be selected from this group later, spend time now and make it the best group possible.

(See Worksheet 2.1, Appendix B.)

PERSONALITIES ASIDE

Sometimes people have a hard time getting past personalities when they try to form a group. Although certain temperaments are difficult to overlook in some instances, occasionally they work for a group in unexpected ways.

For example, one group that I know felt a particular woman was too outspoken at every meeting. She sometimes spoke in an unthinking manner that irritated several other members. However, her alter ego was that she worked wonders for the library in the groups to which she belonged, getting them to help the library in surprising ways and always looking for new ways to bring in that help. She was a good organizer and took responsibility for two successful fundraising events. Members saw her intentions were good and learned to turn her remarks aside with humor.

Another group had doubts about nominating a man to their board because he always seemed to be busy. Could he really take on something more? Well, he accepted the library job, absorbed it into his other interests and represented the library in all of them. Not only that, he was also a crackerjack note-taker and kept the minutes in tidy condition.

Even if you have been to meetings with group members for other ventures and purposes, try to prepare for core group discussions with positive feelings and interest. Take a few minutes when you start the meeting to make sure everyone knows other members, and that you all know a little about one another. Specifically, it would be beneficial to know what drew them to the library project to begin with, what experience or background they have which could be useful. A friendly chat before any meeting warms things up before the major discussions begin.

3

Supplies and
Core Group Meetings

Good supplies are like good tools—they help you do a better job. Good meetings help you save time, learn from one another, and also help you to do a better job.

Supplies for the Core Group

In the case of the supplies I recommend, you may want to purchase some with seed money; I have placed an asterisk after these. I feel it is a perfectly justifiable expense, and some of the things you may need to purchase will be useful to the library later on.

There are some supplies you will recognize as free for the asking and some you may have on hand already.

SUPPLIES TO HAVE ON HAND

- A Roster of Group

  Give everyone a copy at the first meeting. Any communicating between meetings will be facilitated. The list should include full names, addresses and telephone numbers.

- Post Office Box*

  Boxes range from $14–$22 for annual fees

Get a medium to big one if available since you may be receiving catalogues and large envelopes.

You could use a member's own mailbox and number, but a rented box demonstrates permanence:

Sample: Handleberg Library Committee
         PO Box 557 / 609 Main Street
         Handleberg, YS 90003

- *Robert's Rules of Order* *

This book will come in handy if you do not have anyone versed in meeting's dos and don'ts. You will be voting on proposals and making decisions; you don't want to find they are invalid because of incorrect procedure!

Most bookstores have a copy of *Robert's* or will order it for you. Someone can purchase it over the Internet from one of several on-line book sources. Of course, you could borrow a copy from another organization, or even the closest library.

- A Notebook*

Maintain meeting minutes and any other correspondence to and from the group.

A 3-hole style is best as it keeps things in place. Buy dividers for minutes, correspondence, documents created and reports of committees. Place them in those sections in the order they are written, showing date and person responsible.

- Address Book*

Use for addresses, telephone and fax numbers. (Also e-mail addresses if you have access to e-mail.) As you contact people, all information you need about them will be in one place. Jot a note about the person or business to remind everyone why you entered the name in the first place.

Sample: Murray, James
         669-777-3344
         354 First Street
         Printing business/Open 9–6 weekdays. Does posters and flyers.

- Calendar*

You should look for one of those big ones—a year, or a month-at-a-glance. The format should be *large*. Cute pictures are unnecessary; big spaces to write in count here.

- Local and Larger Area Telephone Books

You will be glad you have numbers and addresses for all local agencies, businesses, state and county agencies and newspapers. This will save you time when you want numbers fast!

- Map*

  You need to have a large map of the community or area for posting the busy places in your community when considering the library's possible location.

- Local and County Roster

  These list local, county and state office holders' addresses and telephone numbers, meeting times, and agencies.

- Local Newsletters, Publications and Calendars

  Collect sources for community calendars, local newsletters and newspapers' local new sections. Make sure you keep the parts detailing respective deadlines and fees (if any).

- List of Who's Who at Your State Library

- List of Potential Donors

  Sponsors and partners' addresses, telephone numbers and reason for listing should be kept. Check that supporter list, too!

Meetings for Core Group Sessions

MEETING PLACE

Try to have one place for all meetings. This will eliminate the chance of confusion and missed meetings. Such a location should be easily accessible for all involved. It also can provide a place to keep things used at every meeting. A telephone would be nice, but not absolutely necessary. This may or may not turn out to be the future site of the library you all hope for.

At this stage, do not get talked into renting a place because "it'll be perfect for a library." Rent is an unwanted and unnecessary expense at this point. It might probably not be perfect for the library you have not even planned yet.

Somewhere someone will have a room you can use on a regular basis—a church Sunday school room, a "back room" in someone's home, even a classroom in the school—where you can all meet comfortably and have privacy to get things accomplished. Someone may have to lug all the papers to every meeting, but that is still better than encumbering yourselves with a monthly rent.

Maybe someone has a spare room who will ask only that you keep it clean in exchange for its use. Excellent idea!

SET UP A MEETING SCHEDULE

Decide at your initial meeting when you will meet—Every other week? Once a month? Once a week?

Look up the dates, write them down and give every member a copy. Try not to change dates more than a couple of times.

Keep an Accurate Record

As meetings occur, date each piece of paper connected with the library project. Keep track of who said and did what. In other words: keep good minutes!

Valuable time is wasted when person A thinks person B has done something and Person B thinks the reverse; nothing gets done at all.

We humans like to think we can remember accurately; praise to those who can! For the rest of us who cannot, the recording secretary will take notes and then remind us. I have been known to send minutes to members shortly after a meeting just to make sure things are clear.

Be certain each member knows what their next or ongoing responsibility is at the close of each meeting. Review what was assigned and to whom.

Absenteeism

Back when I spoke about the need for commitment of time, I stressed the necessity of working hard and long, of setting aside other things for the duration. It was sincerely meant and I stress here that if a member misses more than three meetings, you should see if a replacement is needed. People can catch up for just so long before they lose the thread of meaning and sense of direction the other members share.

Here's a story to illustrate my point. I remember having a wonderful group ready to work on a library's long-range plan. We all met the first time and were excited about how much we accomplished. The next time, we met the same thing happened with 100 percent attendance.

The third meeting however, and the fourth, had one person absent on both occasions. Even with giving notes to her, and having discussions between meetings, when she came to the fifth meeting, we all lost time explaining nuances not covered in the minutes. She brought up ideas which had been broached and discarded; time was lost and some other members were frustrated.

She missed the next meeting, so I had to call and ask her if she thought she should continue. Understanding she was not contributing what we both desired, she decided to serve in another way. At the following meeting, the group was fully able to proceed.

While tooting the horn of attendance, I will in the next breath make a bit of an exception: Everyone is entitled to one break in order to refresh and recommit. I intentionally miss one library board meeting a year. I receive a sense of rest and relaxation from playing hooky. My library board members miss no more than two meetings apiece and agree that it makes them all the more ready to come back and continue.

So allow each member of the core group to miss *one or two* meetings and be "off call" (instead of "on call") for a week or so. Chances are they will be back raring to go.

USE THIS BOOK!

Encourage everyone in the core group to read this part of the book. While your core group may decide to use only some sections, I think you will find any and all of it helpful.

You can choose which aspect of the library you want to investigate next: the "nuts and bolts" of creating the library in one place, the planning aspects of the physical library, establishing goodwill in the community and where to go for further information. Since no single chapter hangs on the one before or after it, you can chart your own course.

Have one copy of the book available at meetings, and then at the library, placed so anyone can have access to it. If you've read this far—you are serious, so good luck!

The Library's Role
Within Its Community

Its Role

What is this library's role going to be?

Even if you think you know what library role means, I do not recommend skipping this chapter.

Asking that lead question of a core group usually brings forth the resounding answer: "Why, it's going to be a *library*, of course!"

Yes, it is, but what kind of a library? How will it be defined; i.e. what will be its role? If you are not sure why this is an important question, stay tuned. Once you have defined a library's role, you will use it later when creating the mission statement, the selection policy, donation policy, and other documents.

Here are some of the basic library roles to be considered:

- Popular Materials Center
- Educational and Informational Center
- Educational Support
- Historic and Archival
- Special Collection.

Now, of course you in the core group have to consider which one or more roles describe what you had in mind when you decided to start "a library." Here is something about each one in an attempt to make your job easier.

21

POPULAR MATERIALS CENTER ROLE

Do you see it as a place to borrow good popular materials, periodicals and audio/video materials? If so, there should be a pleasant combination of fiction and nonfiction, with no pretense to be instructional.

EDUCATIONAL AND INFORMATIONAL CENTER ROLE

Does the core group see itself creating a library whose main job will be to provide materials to people doing research, needing reference materials or completing assignments? The collection would include a broad range of subjects (nonfiction materials). Certainly you would need Internet connections plus some good CD-ROM resources.

I asked a core group if they thought they could come up with the funds for such a role, explaining that several areas in educational resources (i.e., scientific, legal, health related, and political changes) must to be kept up-to-date in order to be accurate and useful. I described how school and academic (college and university) libraries handle this role naturally. If you have one or both of those within an easy drive from your town, you probably do not need to adopt this as your primary role.

EDUCATIONAL SUPPORT ROLE

This is a simpler version of the one above. In this role a library works with the local school and supports assignments. Subject areas covered each year are represented in the library's collection. School reading lists can be consulted when purchasing fiction; study areas can be provided in the library; textbooks can be on reserve for evening hours.

HISTORICAL AND ARCHIVAL ROLE

Does the group see a library where historic documents pertaining to the locale are kept and available? Sometimes there is a plethora of local history materials in a community, but nowhere to organize and use them. There could be books, letters, newspapers, records, photographs and artifacts. If there is no historical society already working on such a project, maybe that would be your primary role.

SPECIAL COLLECTION ROLE

Do you see the library as having only one particular category or subject area in its collection? Suppose someone has whispered in a group member's ear that they have a vast collection on marine life, European art, or Mark Twain, and would like to give it outright to a library [should there ever be one]. You may consider the care and preservation of that collection as the basis for your role.

Such a collection would need organization and related elements could be added. For example, in the case of a Mark Twain collection, the library could add information on the Mississippi, river travel and abolition.

I hope that "library role" is a clearer concept to you now; as you discuss and decide which role to adopt, I think the concept will become clearer yet. Such a discussion will also be a good time for all members to describe what they had in mind when they got involved in the first place. (Remember when talking about *interest* in a library, remember that not everyone's interest is the same.)

When discussing the library's role, whether among yourselves and out in public, be careful not to "build castles (or libraries) in the air." Don't make promises or describe plans that may turn out to be impossible to keep and realize. A planning group that blows a lot of hot air about fantastic "wait 'til you see what we're going to do" plans, but doesn't deliver, loses community support and future interest. This may be your only chance to establish support, it may well be impossible to recapture it if once lost.

Moral: It is better to *underplay* than overplay! Keep things basic until things are accomplished and sure.

Now is a good time for expectations to be aired and misconceptions to be straightened. You will then be able to reach a consensus and will have decided the library's role—so have at it!

5

The Core Group's
Mission Statement
and Logo

I have introduced the idea of a mission statement to library boards, and I found they had to be convinced of its importance. "I don't mean to be difficult," one straightforward little lady said, "but why do we need one?" They were surprised when I rubbed my hands in glee and replied, "I'd love to tell you!"

In case some of you mentally asked the same question, here's my explanation—and I still love giving it!

To some people, having a mission statement sounds pompous, as though it's something only big corporations and universities have. Not so. Small church groups often have a mission statement. Your school district has one. Museums have them, and so does Wal-Mart, a "people" business if ever there was one! Some purposes of the mission statement:

- A mission statement puts into words what an organization's purpose is. It expresses their raison d'être, or their guide if you will.
- It holds out that guide as something with which the organization as a whole can align all its work.
- It clarifies for present and future group members what the parameters of the organization are; indeed, it will guide the organization as it develops.

Your mission statement may or may not be the same as the one used later by the library board of trustees. I say "may not" only because it may be so good they will decide to use your mission statement as theirs! In fact the library board may have many, if not all, of the same people on it.

Your job now, however, is different from a board's. Your goal is essentially to get the library open. Their job will be to run the library; their goals will be different within that job. So think in terms of your goal right at this point—don't worry about their later goal and job.

It will help as you discuss among the group what it thinks the mission to be if everyone considers this question: How can we express our library's role? How can we express our library role and our primary goal within that role? Answer that, and you have your mission. For example:

- What is our library role?
- Do we need to find a building for the library, or do we want to build a new one?
- Do we want to have all preliminary paperwork done for the library before it opens its doors?
- Do we want to have all books on the shelf?
- Do we want a bank account of a particular amount?
- Do we want to have a board in place?

Mission statements show intent to do something. Speaking grammatically, it is preferable to use good verbs showing that intent: "The So and So Group will provide…, will create…, will continue…, will encourage…, will make available…, will promote …, seeks to…."

When you have created a simple mission statement, you will have given the group a tool to use as a backboard. Bounce all your ideas for the library off the statement and see if those plans fit within the statement.

If someone outside the group comes to one of you with "a marvelous idea," see if that marvelous idea fits the mission. If not, you have a pleasant and professional reason for not incorporating their idea. Do keep a list of all such ideas for a later time when they might be useful!

For now, though, stick to the agenda of the mission statement; it will save you from wasting time by going off onto unrelated tangents.

Figure 5.1 gives a sample mission statement from a library. This library chose as its primary role that of popular materials center and as its secondary role one of educational support.

(See Worksheet 5.1, Appendix B.)

Figure 5.1
Sample Mission Statement

The _____ Library offers recreational and basic informational materials to the town of _____.

It seeks to serve the town through community assessment, reevaluation of its services and collection, and by cooperative efforts with nearby educational institutions.

In a broader sense, it is available to any and all neighboring areas, and honors other (in-state) library cards; it seeks to serve all borrowers in the best way it can.

_____ Library joins the libraries within the State of _____ to offer and improve services to all who seek them.

Adopted _____ by the _____ Library Board of Trustees.

This mission statement will help keep them within the bounds of their library role, and yet allow them to expand within that role toward the best service they can provide.

By the way, a mission statement is not set in concrete—it can be changed. Indeed it should be reexamined when the community assessment is reviewed to make sure the library is keeping pace with its service area. (See Chapter 7.)

A Project Logo

You've done your share of hard work with the mission statement. Now, I would like you to do one more thing—and this one is fun!

The task is to design a logo for the project. Use it on every piece of paper you send out connected with the planning of the library. When the same logo is used consistently all the way through a project, people connect it to that project automatically: "Oh! This must be about the library. I see the symbol!"

Right—a logo is a symbol, one that in your case will stand for the creation of the community's library—a building, an open door, anything that is attractive and easy to recognize. You can always ask a school art teacher to try a few for you if no one in the core group is artistic or brave enough to try.

In graduate school I did a long and productive internship which entailed doing community assessments for five libraries within a library system. I chose a rather raucous image of buildings (silhouettes) bursting from a curve; to me this said these communities were growing, changing, bursting out of their old profiles and my project detailed how.

I used that logo on every fax, every letter, every chapter heading page, and of course on the covers of each finished product. I even enlarged it and put it on the office door. Soon all the staff at the system knew anything with that logo equaled Community Assessment!

(See Worksheet 5.2, Appendix B.)

The thing to remember about a logo as it is created—keep it simple. Some points to remember about a logo:

- Think in terms of it as an advertisement.
- What do you want people to think when they see it?
- Do you want to have them need to figure out what it is every time? Do you want them to consider it cartoonish?
- Would you rather they think it symbolic of a project which they immediately recognize? (This one wins, of course!)

6

Planning:
Deadlines and Timelines
Are Good for You!

We could refer to a timeline as a short-range plan. That is a good analogy. Drafting a timeline means starting at the end and working backwards. What do you want to get done and by what date do you want it done? In the intervening weeks between "today" and that date, what must occur to get you there?

Each step along the timeline gets the group closer to the goal. In writing short- and long-range plans, these steps are referred to as objectives. Each step and its assignment, or job, has a deadline attached. This keeps things moving forward toward the goal instead of sideways into no-man's-land. The supreme goal, or the end of the timeline, is achieved by steadily taking small steps or objectives. Figure 6.1 at the top of page 30 provides a timeline sample.

Okay. Get the idea? Definite deadlines will help to get things done. If a chairman only says "do it when you can," chances are that the task may never be completed. The chairman should assign all deadlines after discussion within the group.

Use that big calendar I suggested you buy. Write all project deadlines in a particular color which will represent an important deadline!

You can also design a timeline the way they make those wonderful timelines about dinosaur times. You can use a roll of shelf paper and draw it out from beginning to end; this would enable you to see where you have been and where you still have to go. Stretch it all the way across the room, listing all holidays

---

Figure 6.1
Sample Objectives and Proposed Deadlines

Today's Date—December 1999 (for discussion's sake).

What we've accomplished so far: group's formation, list of all interested people, community's expectations and potential in-kind services, group's mission statement.

GOAL: By December 2000, To have all necessary groundwork done and be able to open library doors!

1. 1st Objective—Create a core group and who is doing what, statement of commitment, schedule of meetings: by February 15, 1999.
2. 2nd Objective—Define library role, location for meetings, supplies: by April 1, 1999.
3. 3rd Objective—Complete community assessment and community list: by June 1, 1999.
4. 4th Objective—And so forth

---

and events which everyone knows about and has on their own calendar. Now put in your group's deadlines in relation to those holidays.

The goal, of course, comes at the end. You could even choose a holiday as the goal deadline: "By Thanksgiving, we will…"

This may make things more relative to daily life as you all know it. It may also help to keep things within a realistic time frame and not be overly idealistic.

Figure 6.2 presents an example.

Figure 6.2
Sample Timeline

Today's Date	Valentine's Day	Easter	School Ends	4th of July	Labor Day	Halloween
Deadline	*1*	*2*	*3*	*4*	*5*	*6*
	step	step	step	step	step	step
	who	who	who	who	who	who
	date	date	date	date	date	date

This is as wide as I can make it here, but you can use a much longer piece of paper and go all the way through a year if you wish. You will notice that even with the holidays being listed, I still assign a specific date to each step. I also indicate you should write down who is in charge.

Remember, you have all committed to this project! Having the secretary or chairman call or write to remind people of their deadlines is a good idea, too.

7

Community Assessment:
The Essential Tool

This is a topic I take delight in addressing. Having done considerable work on community assessment, I cannot emphasize too much the importance of doing a good one. Once a library has thoughtfully examined its community and reassessed all assumptions about that community, it can begin to accomplish:

- Good planning
- Appropriate and helpful policies
- Relevant collection development
- Beneficial programming
- Publicity that *targets all segments* of the population.

As the core group, you are representative of the whole community and as such are in a position to draw together information for a profile of that community. If someone in your group says, "Oh, an assessment is the same as a survey," I say, "Attention: This is not just another survey!"

There are some differences between a survey and an assessment.

- A survey asks questions; a community assessment develops a descriptive narrative of a community.
- A survey could be handed out in almost any town; a community assessment describes only one service area—yours.

- The same subject areas are covered in a good assessment (demographic, socioeconomic, geographic, political, educational, health and welfare, information sources, commercial sources available), but each service area will create a unique description.
- Survey questions can find out things like:

What services would you like?
What parts of the collection would you use most?
What hours would be best for you?
Have you used a library before?

An assessment will find out the following about a service area.
- Size of the pre-school age group, the school age group
- Number of single parent families
- 65 and over population, the middle-age group
- Number of people finishing versus not finishing high school; number going on to higher degrees
- Median family income
- Cultural diversity of the population.

It would be most helpful, if you have the time, to compare the last two censuses to learn how those areas have changed. Of course, if the next census is looming large on the horizon, you may want to wait and do a comparison assessment after it is published. I will come back to this "use of two" when I talk about writing the assessment.

Here are the basic steps to a good community assessment.

Gather Factual Information

If you are going to conscientiously serve a larger area, include information about the whole area.

TOOLS

Incorporate several studies into your assessment. These could include:

- The last (two, if possible) U.S. census(es) of service area
- State and county agencies or offices that affect service area

- Local town or village government and organizations (rosters or compiled lists)
- Any local studies (water use, land development, environmental) containing useful figures
- "Accountability Report" (or similar title) from state department of education
- County extension agency list of programs and number of participants in your area (do not ask for names)
- School district superintendent's secretary for special education and free lunch figures
- Your state library statistics on existing libraries for comparison (population of service areas, local financial support)
- Any other fact-based sources that might be unique to your area.

All of the above are generated from your town, the larger service area, the county or the state, and provide valuable (free) information for you.

The U.S. Census

This is an amazing tool: It will give you information on population, education attainment, unemployment, where and how far away people work, cultural diversity, language spoken, median income and how many families there are in your area.

You can locate the U.S. Census on the Internet (http://www.census.gov) or in print form through your county or state government. Your town clerk may have a printout of your geographic area, but you will probably need to get more.

If you ask someone else to send you the information, make certain you give them the census areas you want and need. There are many areas available and you do not want to waste their time or get information you do not need.

Areas of absolute interest to a library trying to examine its service area:

- Population growth, commercial growth (centers)
- Age (define age groups, changes in those groups, trends)
- Work (where, what kind, unemployment)
- Family or households (single; two-parent families; single-parent families; living alone; working parents)
- Income (retired, median wage, poverty)
- Education (school enrollment, educational attainment, degrees, dropouts)
- Cultural diversity (ethnic groups, their trends, languages spoken at home)

- Transportation (walkers, drivers, carpoolers, commuters, public transportation users, time of day people come and go)

Figure 7.1 is a sample from the 1990 United States census (with disguised county name and numbers) to give you an idea of what you'll find.

Figure 7.1
Sample Census Data

1990 U.S. Census Data
Database: XXXXXXXXX
Summary Level: State-County

Handleberg County: FIPS.STATE=**, FIPS.COUNTY**=***

PERSONS	
Universe: Persons	
Total	12,219
FAMILIES	
Universe: Families	
Total	3,442
RACE	
Universe: Persons	
White	11,149
Black	88
American Indian, Eskimo, or Aleut	151
Asian or Pacific Islander	12
Other race	819
PERSONS OF HISPANIC ORIGIN	
Universe: Persons of Hispanic origin	
Total	3,378
FAMILY TYPE AND AGE OF CHILDREN	
Universe: Own children under 18 years	
In married-couple family:	
Under 3 years	280
3 and 4 years	328
5 years	125
6 to 11 years	771
12 and 13 years	309
14 years	140

Figure 7.1
Sample Census Data (continued)

15 to 17 years	340
In other family:	
Male householder, no wife present:	
Under 3 years	31
3 and 4 years	10
5 years	29
6 to 11 years	53
12 and 13 years	14
14 years	14
15 to 17 years	23
Female householder, no husband present:	
Under 3 years	57
3 and 4 years	39
5 years	14
6 to 11 years	195
12 and 13 years	27
14 years	16
15 to 17 years	83
SEX BY MARITAL STATUS	
Universe: Persons 15 years and over	
Male:	
Never married	1,060
Now married:	
Married, spouse present	2,858
Married, spouse absent:	
Separated	75
Other	155
Widowed	90
Divorced	473
Female:	
Never married	692
Now married:	
Married, spouse present	2,914
Married, spouse absent:	
Separated	67
Other	95

(continued on page 38)

Figure 7.1
Sample Census Data (continued)

Widowed	560
Divorced	565

AGE BY LANGUAGE SPOKEN AT HOME AND ABILITY
TO SPEAK ENGLISH
Universe: Persons 5 years and over
5 to 17 years:

Speak only English	1,809

Speak Spanish:

Speak English "very well"	299
Speak English "well"	112
Speak English "not well" or "not at all"	36

ANCESTRY
Universe: Persons
Ancestry specified:

Single ancestry	8,371
Multiple ancestry	2,790
Ancestry unclassified	190
Ancestry not reported	868

MARITAL STATUS BY AGE
Universe: Females 15 years and over
Never married:

15 to 24 years	422
25 to 34 years	126
35 to 44 years	59
45 years and over	85

Ever married:

15 to 24 years	151
25 to 34 years	780
35 to 44 years	881
45 years and over	2,389

PLACE OF BIRTH
Universe: Persons
Native (001-099):

Born in State of residence	5,888

Born in other State in the United States (001–059):

Northeast (009, 023, 025, 033–034, 036, 042–044, 050)	337
Midwest (017–020, 026–027, 029, 031, 038–039, 046, 055)	1,023

Figure 7.1
Sample Census Data (continued)

South (001, 005, 010–014, 021–022, 024, 028, 037, 040, 045, 047)–	3,464
West (002–004, 006–008, 015–016, 030, 032, 035, 041, 049, 053)	915
Born outside the United States (060–099):	
Puerto Rico (072–075)	3
U.S. outlying area (060–071, 076–099)	2
Born abroad of American parent(s)	89
Foreign born (100–999)	498
PLACE OF WORK—STATE AND COUNTY LEVEL	
Universe: Workers 16 years and over	
Worked in State of residence:	
Worked in county of residence	4,659
Worked outside county of residence	358
Worked outside State of residence	60
MEANS OF TRANSPORTATION TO WORK	
Universe: Workers 16 years and over	
Car, truck, or van:	
Drove alone	3,582
Carpooled	827
Motorcycle	21
Bicycle	12
Walked	242
Other means	97
Worked at home	290
TRAVEL TIME TO WORK	
Universe: Workers 16 years and over	
Did not work at home:	
Less than 5 minutes	651
5 to 9 minutes	1,235
10 to 14 minutes	920
15 to 19 minutes	720
20 to 24 minutes	300
25 to 29 minutes	91
30 to 34 minutes	445
35 to 39 minutes	56
40 to 44 minutes	38
45 to 59 minutes	153

(continued on page 40)

Figure 7.1
Sample Census Data (continued)

60 to 89 minutes	133
90 or more minutes	45
Worked at home	290
SCHOOL ENROLLMENT AND TYPE OF SCHOOL	
Universe: Persons 3 years and over	
Enrolled in preprimary school:	
Public school	105
Private school	38
Enrolled in elementary or high school:	
Public school	2,152
Private school	25
Enrolled in college:	
Public school	278
Private school	60
Not enrolled in school	9,153
EDUCATIONAL ATTAINMENT	
Universe: Persons 18 years and over	
Less than 9th grade	812
9th to 12th grade, no diploma	1,354
High school graduate (includes equivalency)	3,003
Some college, no degree	2,230
Associate degree	342
Bachelor's degree	927
Graduate or professional degree	431
INDUSTRY	
Universe: Employed persons 16 years and over	
Agriculture, forestry, and fisheries (000–039)	447
Mining (040–059)	45
Construction (060–099)	455
Manufacturing, nondurable goods (100–229)	70
Manufacturing, durable goods (230–399)	91
Transportation (400–439)	163
Communications and other public utilities (440–499)	151
Wholesale trade (500–579)	122
Retail trade (580–699)	1,137
Finance, insurance, and real estate (700–720)	369
Business and repair services (721–760)	224

Figure 7.1
Sample Census Data (continued)

Personal services (761–799)	351
Entertainment and recreation services (800–811)	175
Professional and related services (812–899):	
Health services (812–840)	452
Educational services (842–860)	370
Other professional and related services (841, 861–899)	225
Public administration (900–939)	335
MEDIAN HOUSEHOLD INCOME IN 1989	
Universe: Households	
Median household income in 1989	19,489
NONFARM SELF-EMPLOYMENT INCOME IN 1989	
Universe: Households	
With nonfarm self-employment income	719
No nonfarm self-employment income	4,042
FARM SELF-EMPLOYMENT INCOME IN 1989	
Universe: Households	
With farm self-employment income	219
No farm self-employment income	4,542
INTEREST, DIVIDEND, OR NET RENTAL INCOME IN 1989	
Universe: Households	
With interest, dividend, or net rental income	1,341
No interest, dividend, or net rental income	3,420
SOCIAL SECURITY INCOME IN 1989	
Universe: Households	
With Social Security income	1,593
No Social Security income	3,168
PUBLIC ASSISTANCE INCOME IN 1989	
Universe: Households	
With public assistance income	301
No public assistance income	4,460
RETIREMENT INCOME IN 1989	
Universe: Households	
With retirement income	773
No retirement income	3,988
MEDIAN FAMILY INCOME IN 1989	
Universe: Families	

(continued on page 42)

Figure 7.1
Sample Census Data (continued)

Median family income in 1989	23,988
WORKERS IN FAMILY IN 1989	
Universe: Families	
No workers	623
1 worker	1,012
2 workers	1,495
3 or more workers	312
PER CAPITA INCOME IN 1989 BY RACE	
Universe: Persons	
Per capita income in 1989:	
White	11,120
Black	7,312
American Indian, Eskimo, or Aleut	4,703
Asian or Pacific Islander	5,535
Other race	6,548
HOUSING UNITS	
Universe: Housing units	
Total	12,622
OCCUPANCY STATUS	
Universe: Housing units	
Occupied	4,789
Vacant	7,833

Isn't this fascinating? There are many other categories available as you will see if you have a chance to search the Internet site.

You can imagine how contrasting two censuses would be helpful. How have these figures changed during the intervening ten years, and what does that tell us about this area? Is the population growing? If, so in what ways? Has the median family income grown—by how much? How have the education figures changed—are more high schoolers finishing or not finishing the four-year program? Are more or fewer people going on to college or beyond? What does this mean for a library? Are more or fewer people working right in town—are the self-employed figures growing?

The other sources of information (county roster, school figures) will all be factual information, too. Make a list, or if you have a computer, a table listing what you find. A sample of a way to do it in list form follows with Figure 7.2.

Figure 7.2
Sources and Their Data

POPULATION:
  1. Most current census
SCHOOL ENROLLMENT:
  1. Most current census
  2. Actual school figures (get from superintendent)
SPECIAL EDUCATION:
  1. Superintendent's figures
THOSE COMPLETING HIGH SCHOOL:
  1. Most current census
  2. Superintendent's figures
FAMILIES USING REDUCED OR FREE LUNCH:
  1. Superintendent's figures
SINGLE PARENTS:
  1. Most current census
  2. State Agency with Assistance to Families source figures
PEOPLE OVER 65 LIVING ALONE:
  1. Most current census
  2. State Agency on Aging source figures
SELF-EMPLOYED IN AREA:
  1. Most current census
  2. State Bureau on Employment source
NUMBER OF RANCHERS AND FARMERS:
  1. Most current census (Farm self-employed)
  2. State Agriculture Department figures

Make Observations About Those Facts

Divide (by areas) the facts to be considered among the core group members. Write up what is learned from these facts, based only on the facts you find. You may wish to use the *two* most current censuses and use comparisons. But if you are using only one census (the most recent) the facts you learn will still be useful as a starting place; you will simply write up how those facts describe your community.

Beware of observations like these: I've lived here for twenty years and I know this community. Most everyone works here in town. They're mostly whites. Everyone finishes high school. Not many go to college. Most folks are employed. There are more men than women.

These are biased opinions and can be dangerous to a real community assessment. They are not based on facts, they are merely assumptions. Clear biased opinions away if they exist in your group. Make believe you are learning about your community as a stranger with good factual information before you. I hope you treat this as an exciting chance to get to really see your community.

Figure 7.3 contains sample observations (accompanied by tables using two U.S. Censuses) lifted from a community assessment I did for a library in 1996:

Figure 7.3
Sample Educational Attainment Table
Based on Sample Census Data

Educational Attainment	Children in public K–12	Number of home or private school students	Enrolled college students*	Number of people with 12+ degree
1980	1,620	(private) 0	166	525*
1990	1,102	(homeschool) 25 (private) 85	294	2,881**
Variance	-518	+110	+128	+2356

*1980 census info says "college"; does not stipulate 2 or 4 or graduate level program.
**includes 2-year, 4-year college, or higher degrees.

Media availability and Educational Attainment	School libraries (media centers)	Availability of technology	Number over 18 with H.S. diploma	Number over 18 without H.S. diploma
1980	no	no	1,381	452
1990	3	yes	1,527	876
Variance	+3	good	+146	+424

Many observations can be made from the above table. Data can be obtained to calculate percentages for using in an assessment.

Since 1980, a 25 percent decrease in the number of K–12 students occurred, taking into consideration private and homeschooled students. Without that consideration, in 1990 the percentage would have been a 33 percent decrease.

Several conclusions from the table show increases since 1980:

- 11 percent increase in people finishing high school
- 4 times the number of people attaining degrees higher than high school
- 77 percent increase in number of people enrolled in college

Will these first three groups have higher expectations of their community's library?

- 3-fold increase in number of homeschool and private school students in service area
- Almost twice as many people in 1990 had not finished high school as had in 1980.

What would people in these groups need to succeed or be motivated?

(*See Worksheet 1.1, Appendix B.*)

Make a List of Recommendations

Recommendations will list all the potential ways a library can fit into this community profile. These ways are how the library will *serve.* The recommendations should flow naturally from the facts and observations; that is their basis; you have not invented them from thin air.

Many librarians or boards conducting a community assessment are faced with changing long established library procedures and services. That is often a tough assignment. You are in the enviable position of creating a new library; you are starting fresh. You are lucky!

You will want to refer to the Interests/Expectations of Supporters' Group List (*Worksheet 1.1, Appendix B*), that your group has prepared. Do you see a relationship between what some people thought they would like in a library, and the assessment observations so far? Let's make some conjectures with hypothetical statistics so you see this relationship.

EXAMPLE 1:

(Observation) 40 percent of graduating high school students continue on to some form of higher learning, and

(Interest/Expectation List) 15 people said they would like a quiet place to study and equipment for typing papers. Bingo!

EXAMPLE 2:

(Observation) 51 percent of all families are headed by single parents with children under the age of 18, and

(Interest/Expectation List) 20 people said they would like family or preschool storytimes. Bingo again!

EXAMPLE 3:

(Observation) There are 200 people over the age of 65 living alone and no senior center, and

(Interest/Expectation List) 20 people said they would like "a place to see other folks."

Recommendations would appear like this sample (again from the community assessment done in 1996) presented in Figure 7.4.

FIGURE 7.4
SAMPLE RECOMMENDATIONS BASED ON
EDUCATIONAL ATTAINMENT TABLE

Based on recommendations (Arranged from Easy to Critical)

1. More people have higher levels of education and may expect better quality materials; in the educational support role strive for accuracy and relevancy of materials.

2. Try to reach all private and homeschooled in the service area to make sure they all know your hours and willingness to help them. Plan a meeting to get them all together for a discussion about the library.

3. A suggestion box for titles or areas of interest should be installed. Suggestions should be reviewed and considered whenever materials for the library are ordered.

4. Consider electronic format for educational support materials. Your state library can help with information about newly introduced technology products. Contact the school librarians; what do they like and use most? Students enrolled in public schools use computers as tools to acquire knowledge; they will expect to use them in their public library, too!

5. Consider the people not finishing high school; can the library affect these figures?

These recommendations suggest ways and reasons for connecting to the community. Some potential recommendations can indicate:

- When to be open (operating hours)
- Where to have the library
- Need for children's programs
- Need for large print books
- Desire for place to sit quietly and read
- The call for a community bulletin board
- Need to take books to people without the ability or means to visit the library
- Certain subjects which the library must have in the collection—health, parenting, homebuilding, basic English and math texts, local history.
- A homework center need

A survey may well be one of the recommendations as you begin to think about ways to use the observations.

There is not one thing you can learn from a community assessment that will not improve the way the library plans, selects, decides policy, creates programs, offers services, involves people, participates in community events, or is perceived by all segments of the whole population area.

8

The Community List: Building Support as You Go

One of the most important things a core group or library board can do is to create a community list. You may not realize the fact yet, but it is something you have already begun, and is a natural companion to the community assessment. The list is updated regularly to keep it accurate and current. It will be an invaluable reference tool for board work now and for library staff later.

Basically, a community list contains all organizations, businesses, information sources, and agencies in the library's service area. Each of those in turn has a contact person listed, with a telephone number and the meeting time if applicable. You already have some material for preparing this list: you have lists of library supporters and community characteristics you made when designing the core group, and the community assessment.

The community list can be organized into groups such as:

- Schools (nursery, public, private, church, homeschool)
- Low-income housing developments or units, however it may be defined
- Communicators (editors and owners)
- Service organizations (adult and juvenile)
- Health facilities (hospitals, nursing homes and their support groups)
- Senior citizen facilities (residential and day care)

- Day care locations for children
- Recreational departments, parks, or programs
- Governing bodies (local and county)
- Churches and their groups
- Clubs (social, service)
- Sports groups
- Agricultural groups and agencies (ranches, vineyards, orchards)
- Historical societies and town historians
- Special interest groups (the arts, writers, museums)
- Community organizations
- Agencies (local, county, state)
- Businesses and professionals.

For every category make a list of all organizations and groups, and acquire:

- Correct name of group and its purpose or interests
- Contact person and phone
- Meeting time and place
- Ideas for cooperation and mutual benefits.

(*See Worksheet 8.1, Appendix B.*)

Now match the community list (with its contact people and information) to the community assessment recommendations to get ideas for cooperation and mutual benefits. Which organizations on the community list correspond in any way with the recommendations? Is there a contact person listed? If so, then you will be ready to get in touch with that person and that organization as the library begins to plan services, programs and fund-raising.

You might group the possible areas of cooperation in this way:

- Schools
- Health facilities
- Connections with senior citizens
- Connections with children and young adults
- Town and village governments
- Service organizations: fire, auxiliary, emergency, historical society
- Businesses and industries (large and small)
- Churches
- Publications in the service area.

Now expand the list by adding in the names, telephone numbers and other information you listed with the organizations as shown in Figures 8.1 through 8.4.

Figure 8.1
SCHOOL CONTACTS

School	Telephone	Buildings	Contact Person	Library On Site
Baird Central School	226-2455	K–3: 274 students	Hal Blue	1
		4–6: 293 students	Liz Red	1
		7–12: 455 students	Bett Onze	1
St. Agnes School (Catholic Church affiliate)	226-8500	85 students	Rose Oz	1
Homeschoolers Homeschoolers Unite!	226-8945	25 students (9 homes)	Bill Dodd	0

Use questions and ideas such as the following when deciding how to connect to schools:

- Who uses the public libraries from these groups (students, parents, principal, librarian, physical education teacher, reading specialists)?
- If many students live far out, should the library adjust operating hours?
- Can you access school library collection during summer and vacations?
- Can you jointly plan for collection emphasis?
- Can Baird Free Library compliment schools' collections?
- Can you help with special projects through reserves and interlibrary loans?
- Invite the school staff to the library for a coffee or tea and program. Register the nonregistered on your site!

Figure 8.2
HEALTH FACILITIES CONTACTS

Facility	Telephone	Contact Person
Baird Medical Center	226-2640	Hal Brown
Women's Health Center	226-3888	Betty Green

For connections to health facilities, consider doing the following:

- Place posters (or flyers) in each other's building. (Make sure open hours are clear.)
- Mention library's resources in health and nutrition fields.
- Can they offer suggestions for other resources?
- What are existing support groups and when do they meet?

Figure 8.3
Senior Citizens Groups and Contacts

Organization	Contact Person	Telephone	Meeting Date & Time
XYZ Senior Citizens Club	Gladys Smearing	226-3448	3rd Wednesday— 6:30 pm

Ideas for cooperating and connecting to the senior center may include:

- Place library flyers and posters! (Make sure open hours are clear.)
- Library can post center's menu and schedule of events.
- List the resources library has to offer of interest to this age group.
- Ask for suggestions for services.
- Can the library place and rotate reading material in the center?
- What interests and areas of concern of age group could the library address?

Figure 8.4
Community Organizations and Contacts

Organization	Contact Person	Telephone	Meeting Date & Time
Baird Chamber of Commerce	Steve Harrison	226-8080	?
Baird Preservation & Historical Society	Barbara Freese	226-2794	?

Write a letter to community organizations and ask if someone from the library may attend a meeting to discuss possible mutual benefits:

- Including the library in town and village "packets" given to interested visitors and potential residents.
- Including the library on any lists of community services and organizations.
- Involving the library in all publicity promotions and celebrations of the town.
- Post notices of all town and organization events in library.
- What the library has available now and what it hopes to have.
- What might organizations need that the library could supply?
- Let the library serve as a survey location in the town.
- Create a centrally located community bulletin board which all can use.
  See where matches can be made between groups you want to reach and the groups (age, interest, locale) listed there. You've already got the names, the telephone numbers and the ideas!

Worksheet for connections between library and those on the community list must include the organization name (for each organization), contact person and telephone number, group meeting time and place.

Keep in mind that all connections should be—as much as possible—mutually beneficial to the library and the organizations. Here are some suggestions to get you going:

- Can the library do a program at their meeting?
- Can a joint project be planned to benefit the community?
- Could their group put up a display in the library?
- Can their group meet at the library once a year?
- What services can the library provide this organization?

See Worksheet 8.2, Appendix B, for making connections beetween the library and those on the community list.

— PART TWO —
LOCATING AND SETTING UP THE LIBRARY

9

Potential Locations: Visibility, Parking and Accessibility

Discussing the library in terms of place and a building is a treat for me. I have seen many small rural libraries and they each have their own personality. What makes one more successful than another is interesting to contemplate and worth talking about for a few paragraphs.

In Chapter 10, I will talk about looking for the building itself, but here let us just think about *where* the library might be in your community.

Library *location* means where the library is placed in relation to the whole area it serves. Here are some questions for contemplation:

- How is your community laid out—is it one street or many streets?
- Do you have a business section where most folks go daily or several times a week—post office, food store, restaurants?
- Where are your town hall, town clerk's office, motor vehicle department office, gas company office, school(s), college, factories?
- Are there one or more subdivisions or developments being considered?

Take out the map of your community (on the Supply List in Chapter 3) and mark the busy locations. All of them are places people need to use or get to on a regular basis. In other words, where is "the center" in your community?

I have seen library planning committees place the library out of town where

57

"the development is occurring." There is a fifty-fifty chance this will work out. I have seen development halted in its tracks by economic depression; the library was then isolated in a field six miles from anything else. I have also seen development continue right up to the library doors, bringing lots of patrons and activity.

Because I am writing this primarily for small rural communities, I advise finding a library site near the center cluster of these busy places. This is especially true if the community has not had a library before. Many people may not know "what to do with one," or what it will mean to them. If they can get to it naturally, the chances of them dropping in are much better. Also, the library will be a subject of great interest to everyone around it—they will see your efforts firsthand and word will get around.

(See Worksheet 9.1, Appendix B.)

Visibility

A library should be in a spot visible to the most casual passerby. Can people see the building as they turn down its street? Even with the best of outside signs, I feel it is important not to hide a library behind another building. A library building that has its own spot along a sidewalk and street can create a bright and attractive image.

I am reminded of a small library I visited which had as its address "13B Ash Street." In getting there I took (according to directions given) "one turn left off Main (at the hardware), down two streets to the right (at the yellow house with the sagging porch), and then—four houses down on the left, take the driveway by the gray house in front and we're right behind that!"

This group had been too eager to open "anywhere," and had taken the first building offered them. It was—as you can imagine—far from the main bustle of town and highly invisible. They had a hard time getting patrons to come because it was too out-of-the-way. Do not let this happen to you!

Parking and Accessibility

People should be able to park safely and get to the building easily. That is a clear statement and I cannot think of anyone who would argue against it. Patrons must feel that they are safe going to and from the library, that they can find a parking place within reasonable walking distance, and that it will not be a problem going to the library. This applies particularly to elderly patrons and those with very young children.

Decide if a potential site has safe and adequate parking with a very obvious way to get to the library door(s). Having to climb steep inclines or walk over uneven ground to reach the library entranceway may curtail visits for some patrons. This is not to say the library group cannot refine or improve the landscape around the library. Doing so takes time and probably money, and now you are in a hurry to open those doors. Try therefore to choose a library site that will pose few immediate inconveniences to all patrons.

(See Worksheet 9.2, Appendix B.)

10

Looking for a Building

People can get very interested and have a lot of advice when they find out you are looking for a building for a library—someone they know has "just the place":

- There's that old store that just needs some work.
- John H. would probably give you a great deal on renting his place next to the Post Office.
- Muriel will give you her mother's house if you just agree never to change the interior.
- I'll give you the building—all you have to do is move it, place it on a new foundation, and you can easily get a short term loan to do that!
- Why don't you just throw up some shelves in the back room of the church—that's all you need anyway!

You will probably be able to add your own examples of helpful input soon. Politely digest all such suggestions and just say, "We'll put that on the list as a possibility."

Here are some things you should be examining as you go look at buildings:

1. Roof—You will not want things getting wet, nor do you want drip-catching buckets standing around for people to trip over.
2. Main Entrance—One that is easy to see, easy to get to, and attractive (or potentially so).

3. Floor and foundation—Must be able to bear the weight of books throughout, not just along the walls. I know one library who had to jack up the entire building when the growing collection caused sagging and splitting of beams. Slab foundations are best.

4. One floor level—This will be better for handicapped accessible considerations and weight bearing.

5. Entranceway—There should not be a lot of barriers to getting into the library. You should consider:

- number and height of steps
- weight of door
- Can at least one entrance doorway be made handicapped accessible?

6. Wiring—It should be up to code and have plenty of outlets and fixtures.

7. Restroom(s)—There must be one and it should function properly, even if only for staff. If they are public, they must meet Federal regulations for the handicapped.

8. Open interior—The building should be as open as possible so you are not constrained by a lot of existing walls or tiny rooms when designing a library floorplan. The fewer walls and barriers, the better someone at the desk can see around the library!

Don't these all sound like critical things to consider? Remember, you are trying to save yourself time and effort in an attempt to meet your deadline for opening the doors. Most of your effort should be spent on setting up the library and maybe sprucing up the interior and entranceway. As support and interest increase, you can go back and do other fixups. You do not want to saddle yourselves now with expensive things like installing wiring, putting in a bathroom, or laying new foundations.

There is another financial factor, of course, and that is whether or not the building is free to you. If free, you're all set, and I urge you to seek this kind of arrangement.

Approach owners of available buildings with your mission statement, your bylaws, your community assessment, your timeline and all other plans. This will show them that you are serious in your endeavors.

Try to negotiate a two to three year agreement. For that time period, he or she agrees to let you have the building and you agree to maintain open hours and serve the public.

Be convincing in your belief that a library will enhance the community. This is another reason I urged you to have a group and board that represents the whole community!

If this is a successful approach, make sure all agreements are in writing and approved by someone with legal knowledge. Both parties will thus be protected and no misunderstandings will spoil the goodwill. The following example in Figure 10.1 will give you ideas.

Figure 10.1
SAMPLE LOAN AGREEMENT

Roger Bacall loans free and clear for one year, beginning August 1 , 1999, and ending July 31, 2000, the property at 105 North Anderson Avenue to Handleberg Library Committee. This committee shall use the property for the Handleberg Library, and will maintain the grounds and the interior for that period of time. The library will be open the advertised hours, and will serve the whole community. Roger Bacall agrees to maintain the roof and plumbing of the building and not to sell the property at 105 North Anderson Avenue until the end of this agreement.

This agreement can be renewed and renegotiated in writing no later than sixty days prior to its ending date; after that it will be considered to be automatically renewed.

Signed: (Library Board President)   Date

Signed (Roger Bacall)   Date

Witness(es)   Date

If a rental property presents itself, do not be talked into renting a place because someone else thinks it's a good deal; they are not taking responsibility for the library. If, however, you are strongly attracted to a rental property (remember the previous inspection list), *be aware*:

- A rental or for sale property could still be on the market while the library is in it. In the event that it is sold, you might have to vacate in a hurry.
- Make sure the owner has clear ownership to the rental property. You don't want his problems to affect the library's future.
- Do not sublet a property from someone else.
- Make sure the rent is low, low, low! I cannot urge this enough. To start off with the overhead expense of monthly rent is a heavy burden.

Negotiate a rental agreement with the landlord (Figure 10.2) that is similar to the free loan agreement (Figure 10.1).

Figure 10.2
SAMPLE RENTAL AGREEMENT

Roger Bacall agrees to rent for one year, beginning August 1 , 1999, and ending July 31, 2000, in the amount of $75.00 per month, the property he presently owns at 105 North Anderson Avenue to Handleberg Library Committee.

This committee shall use the property only for the Handleberg Library.

The committee will maintain the grounds and the interior for that period of time, and may be permitted to make cosmetic changes to the interior. There will be no structural changes made without express permission of owner.

The committee will hold and show liability insurance for occupants and building's contents.

The committee agrees to give 60 days notice if it wishes to vacate the property.

Roger Bacall agrees to maintain the building's exterior, roof and plumbing. He agrees and will show proof of insurance on the building and property.

He agrees to give 60 days notice if this property at 105 North Anderson Avenue is sold.

Receipts will be given for all rents by owner to Handleberg Library Committee.

This agreement can be renewed and renegotiated in writing no later than sixty days prior to its ending date; after that it will be considered to be automatically renewed.

Signed: (Library Board President)   Date

Signed (Roger Bacall)   Date

Witness(es)   Date

11

Choosing Library Areas: How Many and Which Ones?

The main and most familiar parts, or areas, of a library are as follows:

1. Checkout desk and information area
2. Work and storage area for staff to process books
3. Children's section (usually for babies through sixth grade students)—picture books and storybooks, first readers, easy chapter books, board books for babies
4. Fiction—adult—novels: mysteries, science fiction, historical novels, espionage, Westerns, horror, suspense
5. Nonfiction—children
6. Nonfiction—adult

   Examples of nonfiction: science, history, health, diet, gardening, biography, travel, religion, philosophy, psychology, occult, antiques, arts and crafts, architecture, agriculture, farming, wildlife, pets, film, drama, great literature
7. Young adult (that mysterious age group somewhere between Sweet Valley High and Gore Vidal)—Sometimes this includes both fiction and nonfiction of particular interest to this age group, with periodicals and videos.

8. Reference (not for circulation)
9. Encyclopedias, dictionaries, almanacs, telephone books, law books, directories
10. Video
11. Audio book
12. Periodical
13. Paperback (adult)
14. Computer area
15. Study area
16. Place to sit peacefully and read newspapers
17. Bulletin Board / announcements / handout area.

Whew! There are more library "parts" than meet the casual eye. How do you decide which ones to include and then how to best arrange them?

It is my belief that libraries have all of the parts listed above, although there may not be a separate physical section for each one. Some are easily and happily placed together as in the following way:

• Every library will have a checkout area with a desk or counter. That's a given. The bulletin board/ announcements/handout area could certainly be adjacent to the desk area. I do not recommend placing announcements and handouts on the desk however—this leads to clutter and confusion. A small table and a bulletin board suspended behind the desk should work.

• A staff work area is important and shouldn't be put in the "we'll figure it out later" column. There will always be jobs for desk staff and other volunteers to attend to (my staff says they never sit around any more!): sorting books, processing books, making cards, filing cards, preparing displays. In order to keep clutter and confusion away from the desk, there needs to be a designated work place. If there is a back room already in existence, that could work, but at least provide a good-sized corner or wall section for a work table, two chairs and storage cabinets for supplies.

• Study and reference, reading areas, newspapers and periodicals—one area with one table and chair set, and a couple of "comfy" chairs with end table.

• Audio book, videos, paperbacks—one area (carousel racks?)

• The children's area can combine nonfiction books and picture books, juvenile novels, etc.

- Young adult materials can be shelved with the adult fiction and nonfiction more easily than into the children's section.
- *OR* keep young adult separate.

As you can see, we have gone from 18 sections to six or seven. If you consider that a more manageable number with which to create a floorplan, I agree with you! As you consider these areas, make sure to leave enough "move around" space—you do not want people tripping over one another, or disturbing someone studying. (See Worksheet 11.1, Appendix B.) Pay particular attention to the entranceway and desk area—so many of us tend to cram as much "stuff" in that area as we can and risk making it difficult to enter and leave without working one's way through a crowd.

12

The Building:
Entrance, Floor Plan,
Furniture and Lighting

Once you have selected a building, you now can begin to physically bring the library to life; you are setting a tone.

Try answering these questions:

- What "hits you" first when you initially enter an unfamiliar library?
- Could you "read" the shelves once you were inside?
- How hard or easy was it to find the library area you wanted (fiction, children's, etc.)?
- Where was a restroom when you needed it? Was there one?

If you feel these questions are foolish, rest assured that subconsciously we all ask and answer them when we first walk into a library that is unfamiliar to us. After all, we are library lovers and have at some point in our school years, careers and leisure sought the library for specific and nonspecific reasons. When we travel, some of us (like me) cannot resist visiting the local library to compare it with others in our repertoire. I do not like to appear stupid—I get frustrated and embarrassed when I cannot find the nonfiction section, for example. I almost always need the restroom while I am in a library (also museums!) and like to easily see a sign directing me there.

69

Now you are in a position of bringing to life a whole new library—where others will visit, stay to browse, or return again and again.

Entranceway

An entrance is more than just a door to walk through. In public buildings—such as a library—the entranceway as viewed from the street may include the sidewalk or path leading from the street or parking lot, the steps, the doorway itself and perhaps a vestibule with a second set of doors.

Many libraries miss a chance to boost their image in the community by allowing an entryway or doorway to grow shabby, with steps not swept clear, or windows grown dirty. These things can happen if you pass by them day after day and do not see them from others' perspective. Try to approach the library with a stranger's eye and see how it looks. If it is unattractive—spruce up the place!

It has been said of houses that the hallway sets the tone for the rest of the home. The entranceway gives a clue to what can be found beyond. Whatever the library's point of entry, give it the best appearance you can. These things can make a difference:

- Sign identifying it clearly as a library
- Good and safe lighting if there are operating hours after dark
- A legible announcement of hours
- Friendly signs—*do* welcome people; *do not* emphasize the negative (what cannot be done or what is not allowed).

When you have tended to these things, go outside. Approach the library as a stranger and see if you recognize it as a library, can read the signs from the street and feel as though you would like to visit.

Upon entering the library, whether it is into a vestibule or into the library itself, there should be a sense of quiet order. Do not serve confusion to patrons when they first enter.

The desk should be neat and ready for business. An attractive piece of art or single sign is good. A simple holder for bookmarks or flyers would be fine, too. Do not have food, handbags, coats and other personal items lying about.

Floor Plan

Sometimes people just move shelves around until "they fit" and say they are done arranging the library. I encourage you not to lay out your library that way, and here is why.

You should *plan* the layout of the library, no matter how temporary the quarters might be. Make a simple drawing of the available floor space as in Figure 12.1, showing the permanent walls and fixtures in your building. Include existing weight-bearing walls and other permanent parts of your library building, such as doorways, pillars and windows. They are the limitations placed on you, and you cannot change them—especially if you are renting (see sample agreements, Figures 10.1 and 10.2, Chapter 10). Place your library areas list beside this drawing (see Chapter 11). You are now ready to create the floor plan.

A carefully thought out floor plan creates a wonderful sense of order in a library. There can and should be a natural flow between areas; after all, there is a natural relationship between some of them. Take a look at those library areas that you settled on. Do you see, for instance, why you might want to have the children's section within sight and not right next to the quiet reading area? Certainly it might be fine to put the computer/study area next to the adult fiction (not a whole lot of ruckus occurs in either!) The nonfiction could be near the study area, too. The young adult section—if you decide to include one—should have a little privacy; that age group appreciates it. So do not put it right next to the desk or the children's section! However, if it was beside the adult fiction or paperback areas, the readers might naturally gravitate into those interest levels and authors.

Now, cut a piece of paper into as many areas as your list has; just small rectangles will do for now, as shown in Figure 12.2.

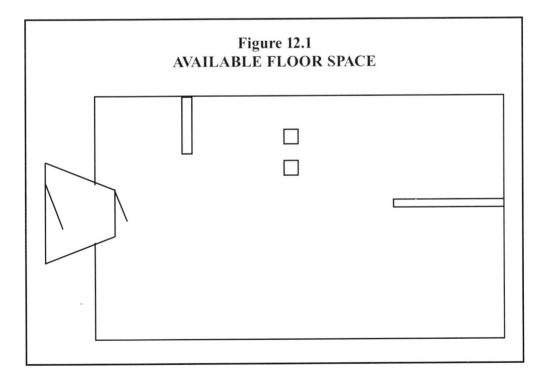

Figure 12.1
AVAILABLE FLOOR SPACE

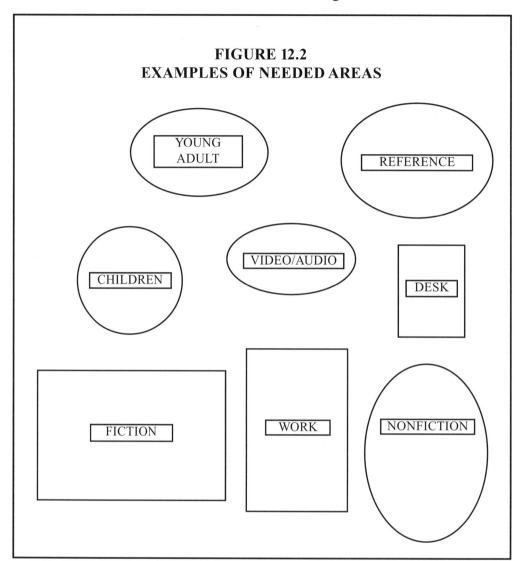

FIGURE 12.2
EXAMPLES OF NEEDED AREAS

Areas may overlap as you place them. This is just to give you an idea of relationship and a traffic pattern. Move things around until you have what you think will work. Try to imagine actual people moving into and then around the floor space. The only caution I will offer is not to crowd the entryway or the circulation desk; people will be going in and out and standing at the desk all at the same time. Leave plenty of room to do all three!

(See Worksheet 12.1, Appendix B.)

When you have the areas arranged in an agreed upon design, you can then imagine how they will stretch out toward and into one another. In this way, they bring about their own borders: solid (by walls, partitions or shelving), or implied by furniture arrangement.

Shelving

There is ideal library shelving, and then there is the shelving most volunteer libraries start with: whatever they can get that is cheap, if not free. Probably you will take what you can and be glad to have it. I would like to encourage you to aim a bit higher, though, and try for shelving that will be really useful.

Good library shelving is adjustable, so it can be moved up or down to fit the size of the books it holds. Picture books and many nonfiction books come 12 to 14 inches tall and need that height to be shelved so their spines are facing out. Adjustable shelving is usually metal, and may have metal or refinished wood ends. It can be single-faced, or double-faced (back-to-back shelves), and can be seen in most large public libraries and in university libraries. Many ready-made types of shelving available at large discount stores are adjustable to a point. One volunteer library was able to get free metal shelving from a local discount pharmacy that was moving to larger quarters.

My second recommendation for shelving material is wood. Ideally, have wood shelves built to your specifications. Each shelf should be about 13 to 14 inches high (with no overhanging lip) and about 9 to 10 inches deep. Have a carpenter advise you on length of shelf after he understands how the weight of books can add up. There is nothing sadder than new wooden shelving suffering from swayback because of the weight of the books on one shelf.

While it would be wonderful to have adjustable or built-to-order wooden shelves, we need to face the fact that most of us in the volunteer library will not start with either type. Because we want to get the library open and have little or no money to purchase shelves (and no local store happens to be getting rid of shelving), we will start with the "what we can get" variety of shelving.

Here are three ways to spruce up the appearance of hand-me-down shelving:

- Paint all shelves the same color. I have seen several varieties of orphan shelving transformed into an orderly family by a universal coat of good gray paint. The library where they were used took on a new, professional appearance, and patrons and staff alike were pleased by the effect. It is a simple thing which makes a big difference.
- Attach good and consistent identification signage to the shelving. I talk about the importance of good signage later, and will only mention here that consistency is the key: the same style of lettering and color background for identical functions, particularly on shelving.
- Create units by standing a low shelf on top of another low shelf. The unit should be checked to make sure it is secure and will not tip over. When

painted the uniform color and displaying signage, it becomes a handsome addition.

For children's books, there are several very creative alternative book cases that you may want to consider installing:

- A number of (sanded!) wooden crates or boxes attached together to form a book house: each "room" contains a letter of the alphabet or particular sets of books. I am thinking of such sets as Golden Books, the Beginning Readers, board books (for babies), the shape books, book sets such as the Berenstain Bears, and others. I used an old, very large dollhouse in one library to hold the Golden Books and Berenstain Bears sets. The children loved it! The attic had a peaked roof where character animals and dolls lived. The whole thing was about four feet tall with a pillow on the floor in front. Have someone put a peaked roof on the book house for added charm.
- Colorful plastic crates can also hold some of these book groups. Each crate must be labeled, though, so books can be easily reshelved. In the juvenile novel section, these would be good for the *Nancy Drew*, *Hardy Boys*, *Choose Your Own Adventure*, *Sweet Valley High*, and other beloved series.
- Sometimes carousels can be found to hold many of the children's series. Book stores or video stores may be getting rid of their old carousel racks. These can be painted in colors complimentary to the basic shelving color and childen can be taught to turn them carefully. There may be other standing wire racks out there too—at hardware or grocery stores or wherever display racks are used.

Put on your thinking caps and go on a shelving Treasure hunt.

Furniture

Aside from shelving, there are other furnishings a Library needs to have. When I talk about furniture later, I suggest that you make a list of what you will need. I repeat here the need to have everything clean (and cleanable), sturdy so it is safe (it will get a lot of use), and easy to fix or tighten should it loosen.

Here are my "furniture" suggestions:

- A good desk, table or counter to serve as the circulation desk. It would be handy if it had at least one drawer for pens and small items, and a file drawer for either letter- or legal-size hanging files and folders. The desk top should be big enough to do the business of checking things in and out without becoming confusing and cluttered.

- A second table or desk can be placed perpendicular to, beside or behind the desk for the telephone, stacks of books ready to be put back on the shelves and other chores connected with running the desk. This keeps the library checkout and library daily chore areas separate and clearly defined.

- A sturdy swivel chair with back support for the people at the desk. The swivel element allows for easy turning and rising when the staff member goes to help patrons.

- Try to have at least one comfortable chair where people can sit and read. Two chairs would be nice, and you can create a setting for these near the magazines and newspapers. These will no doubt be upholstered, so remember to check for cleanliness and odor. I do not think it is looking a gift horse in the mouth—or in this case, a gift chair in the cushions—to check to make sure people will *want* to sit in it!

- Comfort in the children's area may be a big pile of *washable* pillows, or a small table with stools or chairs. I have even seen a small rowboat set right in the middle of the children's area (a good-sized area, to be sure) where kids could pile in with books and stuffed "buddies" to read away the afternoon. Reading lofts covered in carpet can be easily built into corners where space allows. Beanbags make good loungers for children and young adults. I left one whole shelf empty of books in a particularly deep bookcase I had been given; I placed a (*washable*) foam cushion in it and children loved to crawl inside, claiming it as their "reading hole-up." Kids tend to make themselves comfortable anywhere with little assistance from us, however, so do not worry too much about them.

- One or two small end or coffee tables would be fine, if you have room. These allow space for people to set their handbags and other items down while they read or visit. They are also good places to distribute newsletters or small announcements you want people to notice.

- A coat rack or wall rack for outer garments is a must if you live in a climate where winter means coats, mufflers, hats and gloves. Sometimes two racks are a good idea—one regular height for adults and one lower for children. Even for mild climates, it is nice to have a place to hang backpacks,

sweaters and whatever patrons do not want to lug around as they browse
or do research.

- You may want a boot tray for the mud and snow that comes in with the
patrons.
- Of course, most people keep their bad weather footgear on these days. You
will want to find a good-sized mat for foot-stamping use at the entrance,
and another for right in front of the desk where the drips accumulate.
- A table with two, three or four chairs around it provides a place to study
or look through larger books. Remember to check for sturdiness and
repairability—screws that can be tightened, and so forth—for these will
get a lot of use. Metal or wooden tables and chairs are fine—always check
for splinters or burrs—and make sure they are sturdy but not too heavy to
move!
- A couple of wastebaskets are a necessity.
- A small cupboard or storage container for cleaning supplies could be kept
in the bathroom.
- For the staff work area (or if you are lucky enough to have a workroom),
there should be at least one large work surface and some storage shelves.
The inexpensive metal shelves are fine for this area; they will hold supplies, books waiting to be processed and other tools of the trade.
- An under-the-counter refrigerator is a kindhearted addition for the staff
who will be working all day. This can be considered a luxury (adds to the
electric bill), but keeping food cool is a healthy, sensible idea.

While getting furniture to add to the tone of a library is not as easy it was
with the shelving, it still can be done. Chairs and seats can be recovered, wood
and metal can be painted or polished, and you do not need to acquire them all
at once. Start with what you really need (the desk and the shelving) and add from
there. If there is someone in the community who just loves going to garage sales
and has a flair for interior decoration, describe what you would like and corral
him or her into finding it.

Do not be forced into using what may turn out to be a headache. You should
let it be known that if things are donated and you do not or cannot use them, they
may be sold to make money for the library, if the donor does not want them back.
Furnishing a library creatively from scratch can be fun and rewarding: keep that
in mind and I am sure you will enjoy yourself.

Lighting

Inside and outside the library facility, lighting should be adequate. Adequate for young and old eyes, adequate for safety, and adequate to allow folks to find what they are looking for. Young eyes may see pretty well in gloom, but older eyes do not and you want to avoid accidents and the frustration of not being able to see the shelves and book spine labels. Good lighting brightens up the inside, and outside it provides safe passage from the library to parking lot or car.

I have heard staff say they leave the lights off until someone comes in. ("Saves on electricity.") I tell them to turn lights on when they open up in the morning. When lights are on it means "open for business." People looking in from the street will see that the library is indeed open and ready for them. Lights off or turned down confuse patrons—is the library open or not? Are the lights off because the electric bill *didn't* get paid?

At closing time, leave one interior light on for the night, illuminating enough of the floor space to make it difficult for anyone to enter at night and do mischief.

While florescent lighting is the cheapest for ceiling fixtures, it can also be stressful on eyes. Many people (I, for one) get headaches in its presence and begin to feel ennervated. Track lighting can be expensive and tends to only "spot light" narrow areas. If the building you choose has lighting which illuminates *all* areas enough to start with, leave it in place. If not, go to a lighting fixture store and talk to a friendly salesperson who can advise you on inexpensive, nonstressful ceiling fixtures.

Standing or floor lamps in the reading areas would be aesthetically pleasing and would give good reading light to those seated. Be careful of trailing cords, though, and make sure all outlets are safe.

You may want to find a sponsor for this part of the library building project—someone who could cover the cost of purchasing fixtures and any installation involved. If this is the route you take, impress on the potential sponsor the importance of good lighting and how he or she will be remembered every time you flick a switch!

13

Signage:
Inside and Outside

When using the term "library signage," I am talking about the ways and means of identifying the library—its hours, its entrance, its interior areas, its news, its rules and whatever else might be useful to the patrons. There is important signage outside the library and there should be adequate and useful signage inside the library.

While I could just give you a list of signs to make and where to put them, I would like you to understand a few underlying principles of good signage; they hold true for even a small rural library:

- Placement—where it is placed
- Clarity—legibility
- Consistency—in placement, appearance and purpose.

Outside Signs

PLACEMENT

Many public buildings, including libraries, place the sign bearing the library's name flush against the front of the building. Time or money can be spent laboriously carving or painting the name, but when placed above the door (with great pride!), the sign may not be seen from either the sidewalk or the street.

People finding the library for the first time *need to see its sign as they approach*. It would be prudent to have an exterior sign placed perpendicularly: to the street, to the building itself, on the lawn or hung on a post in front. Ask yourself from how many directions will people approach the library—will they see a sign identifying the Library as they get closer?

Not only do you want the library sign to be seen easily, but also the operating hours and the entrance sign (if the building has more than one door) must be clearly visible. People wanting to know when they can use the library will appreciate being able to find out without straining their eyes or walking far to do it. Test the "OPEN HOURS" sign yourself from a spot where others might. Can you read when the library is open? An OPEN/CLOSED sign is helpful but is not enough to give the more important information of when the library is open.

When a building has more than one doorway, people often approach the one which is not the public entrance to the library. Perhaps there is a staff entrance, or a doorway that leads immediately into a meeting room. Going in the wrong way can be embarrassing or inconvenient. Therefore I advise having a statement of ENTRANCE. While this may sound silly to some people, I can attest to going in the wrong way on numerous occasions and being mighty embarrassed by interrupting a meeting which did not involve me!

Place exterior signs thoughtfully, and patrons will find you easily; they will not suffer frustration and will enter the library's public entrance in good spirits!

CLARITY

Clarity refers to the legibility, or readability of exterior signage. *Sacrifice art (fancy lettering or cute symbols) for clearness of message*. Of course, signs can be artful and clear at the same time, and if you can get both, go ahead!

In the case of the library sign, you really only need the name and maybe the year it was established. When you have decided on the perpendicular placement for the sign, decide also on the size of the lettering. Take a stroll through town and see which lettering is visible and clear; measure the lettering for height and width. It can never be too big. If it is too small, it will be wasted effort and could also be wasted expense.

For the OPEN HOURS and ENTRANCE sign, the same rules apply: never mind fancy lettering and resist having cartoon characters or other clever additions. You are simply telling people when you are open and which is the right the door to use.

Keep it big enough, keep it simple, and it will have clarity.

Compare the lettering styles in Figure 13.1.

Figure 13.1
Lettering style examples

HANDLEBERG LIBRARY

HANDLEBERG LIBRARY

HANDLEBERG LIBRARY

HANDLEBERG LIBRARY

HANDLEBERG LIBRARY

Discuss which is the most legible for its placement outside the Library and its readability from some distance.

CONSISTENCY

Consistency in signage refers to the repetition of placement, appearance and purpose. People begin to associate sign styles with the kind of message they carry.

Think for a minute of all the *Special!* sale tags that get used in a food store. Or the *Marked Down!* flags on clothing racks. Or the *Reduced for Clearance!* stickers we find everywhere. Those red or bright orange colors translate into *SALE!* We learn quickly to recognize their message by appearance.

Another example of consistency is when we look up at the overhead signs at the ends of store aisles to find which aisle we want; it is in that location that we know we will find descriptions of what is down that particular aisle.

In exterior Library signage, consistency is simpler than in interior signage. With the exception of the large Library sign itself, the few exterior signs that you will have should all be the same kind or design of lettering. This is not the time to experiment with someone's talent to see how many kinds of lettering they can do. The OPEN HOURS and ENTRANCE signs should be the same simple style. If you need to add PARKING HERE, or MEETING ROOM THIS WAY or any other exterior directional signs, use the same style of lettering.

Figure 13.2 provides examples.

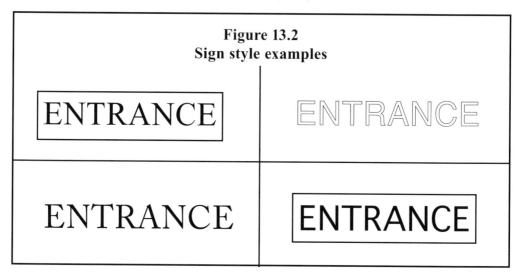

Figure 13.2
Sign style examples

These four style samples of lettering show how different styles can display your exterior messages. They need to be readable, consistent, and placed so all will see them. Which style fits the bill best? Experiment with others; both hand lettering or commercially purchased lettering can work.

(See Worksheet 13.1, Appendix B.)

The Entryway

I call this the "entr'acte" of places for signage: A patron might come into an entryway or vestibule after coming from the parking lot (or sidewalk)and actually going inside the library's interior. There can be a great temptation on the part of staff to post notices all over this vestibule area. How many times have we entered a public building and been visually bombarded by all sorts of large and small notices? Do we even know where to begin digesting them?

Confine notices in the vestibule or entryway area to the most impending current event in the library's life: the upcoming book sale, the announcement of the week's film, the agenda for this week's board meeting, and so forth. I have seen an easel used for this kind of news using attractive, *simple* lettering for the one notice. This combination gives the notice good placement, clarity, and consistency.

If the vestibule is large enough for a bulletin board, that will be a useful place for other notices; I will talk about bulletin boards in Interior Signage.

Interior Signage

While we will apply the principles of good signage inside the library as well as outside, we also need to mention two excellent reasons for good signage

1. It helps patrons feel at home and be more independent as they try to find what they want. Many patrons are reluctant to show they need help.
2. It identifies the library areas for the staff who reshelve material. In the case of a volunteer staff who may not yet be "library trained," this is extremely important and helps avoid muddled shelving.

I believe these reasons speak for themselves to anyone interested in connecting patrons with the materials they seek and in keeping the shelves in good order.

Putting signs up in a library sounds deceptively easy. Do not be fooled. And do not be frightened either. Creating useful signage is fun and makes good sense; you will enjoy the job! It is more fun if you do it in advance of a crisis, instead of in a panic.

Many times libraries—large and small—open their doors and don't think about signs until people begin to ask for the same directions over and over. I would like to suggest that if we put signs up before the library is opened, people are helped rather than frustrated or embarrassed.

I once said to someone who was standing still, gazing around a small library, "You seem to be stumped—can I help you?" "Well," she answered, "I know there must be a local history section but I just cannot seem to see it." There was no reason why she should have found it because there was no sign in sight directing her to its location: back wall, to the left. Of course, at this point, someone scrambled about and taped a quickly handwritten LOCAL HISTORY sign at the end of the appropriate shelving unit.

Then there was the fellow following the alphabet (authors' last names in the fiction section), looking for the P's section. At the L's, the shelving ended and there was no arrow or information about the fact that one needed to go around the corner past the magazine rack to continue. He went to the desk and asked if they had authors after L. Another sign hastily made was taped to the L-shelf giving directions!

Children may not think you own any *Nancy Drew*, *Baby Sitters' Club* or *Choose Your Own Adventure* series if you don't use a sign to tell them "JUVENILE SERIES HERE," with a list and an arrow. Likewise, staff—with no sign to remind them—may shelve those same books by their authors instead of in the designated series area.

For interior signage, you may have someone volunteer to make all of the signs. Great! Just make sure:

- He or she is provided with the list of signs and their sizes, lettering and colors agreed upon.
- He or she understands the principles of good signage.
- All signs of similar use will be lettered the same way (all caps or not, and so forth).
- Good markers, ink and paint are used for clarity and professional look.
- Size of lettering is considered for patrons with varying levels of eyesight.

When the above is written, you have created a signage policy which you will want to refer to as new signs are needed or old ones replaced.

(See Worksheet 13.2, Appendix B.)

Signage's Subtle Message

Be aware that signage can give a subtle or unintended message. "Good" signage truly emphasizes the positive, "bad" signage can emphasize the negative and turn people off. Try not to overuse DO NOT and NO; this puts the negative first.

Figure 13.3 shows some positive signs with their negative relatives.

Figure 13.3

PLEASE LEAVE ALL FOOD AND DRINK OUTSIDE—THANKS

NO FOOD AND DRINK ALLOWED

RETURN YOUR BOOKS HERE

DO NOT RETURN BOOKS HERE

PLEASE ACCOMPANY YOUR CHILD IN THIS AREA

NO CHILDREN ALLOWED BEYOND THIS POINT

PLACE BOOKS HERE FOR RESHELVING—THANK YOU

DO NOT RESHELVE BOOKS YOURSELF

Do you see the difference? I know of one library whose first notice addressing the entering public is: NO LIBRARY CARDS ISSUED WITHIN FIFTEEN MINUTES OF CLOSING. What a warm welcome! It probably sprang up out of staff frustration, but its negative message, placed right by the entranceway, is offputting.

Remember that while most patrons "know the rules," there are those first-time patrons who may get a negative impression of your library through its signage—whether it is negative in tone (DO NOT PLACE BOOKS HERE) or inadequate in its information (BOOKS HERE).

Having said all that, what signs do libraries—even small ones—really need?

GROUP A
Library Areas and Card or Electronic Catalogue

- Overhead is a good location for these as little else should interfere with seeing the signs. If yours is a one-room library, they could be placed on or above the very top shelves (if these are not being used to hold books). Place signs identifying the children's section where both parents and children will see them.
- On the shelves themselves, indicate where the alphabet (for fiction) or numbering system (for nonfiction) starts and which way to proceed. Periodic reminders are wonderful "helps" to people. You can place numbers and alphabet letters anywhere you feel someone may ask the questions "Where am I?" or "Where do I go from here?"
- Keep lettering and numbers simple and uncluttered. Patrons are not interested in artistic style; they want to find something fast!
- Choose dark lettering on light background combinations—the eye can decipher them more easily than light lettering on a dark background.
- Arrows are helpful in directing people at junctions: to the left or right, straight ahead or even around-the-corner.
- Choose a color for background and a straightforward lettering style for this category. People will associate this color and style with directions for the collection.
- In the children's section, identify picture books, juvenile novels, juvenile nonfiction, easy readers, board books, and any other types of books at the exact place they are located. This helps parents, children and staff. Within the children's section, signage could have its own color and style.

GROUP B

Restroom (if Public), Exits, Stairways and Meeting Rooms

- Locate these signs immediately to the right of the doorway that you are identifying, about five feet from the floor. Signs placed on doors are of no use once the door is propped open.
- Choose a color background, strong lettering style, and good size for these.
- Regulation exit signs could, and probably should, be purchased commercially. These are *safety features*.
- Commercial restroom signs (with male/female symbols) will work, too; if one restroom serves both, say so in the sign!
- Arrows should be used for clarification at junctions or corners—wherever confusion might occur (around the corner, down the hall).

GROUP C

Library Policies and Announcements

The policies should be displayed in a prominent place with close proximity to the circulation desk for everyone to see, including the staff. The ones I recommend for this are:

- Confidentiality Policy
- Borrowing or Loan Policy
- Internet Use Policy.

Some libraries frame these in inexpensive frames. Because they are important, they should be easy to read, so do not use fancy, flowing, script lettering. If there is another policy you want the public to see, place it with these using the same lettering and method of display.

All *announcements* should be consistently posted in a place people will get in the habit of checking as they come and go. Such announcements here might be:

- Library fund-raising events
- Request for more volunteers
- Program events
- Questions for patrons
- Book lists
- Changes in schedule or Closings.

Placement of these can be a frustrating exercise; oftentimes we are amazed how people can walk right by signs that we think are perfectly obvious! It sometimes seems no matter where you post library notices, people miss them. Is it them or is it us?

Relax, do the best you can, and after a time most people will find the news you want them to find. I have a hearty suspicion that there are some people who just would prefer you to tell them everything orally—so they ignore all signs on principle!

A bulletin board on legs, placed near the desk, is an excellent vehicle and location to try. Limit the notices to two or three at a time.

GROUP D

Public Bulletin Board

If you have the room, a community bulletin board is a nice service to offer. Because you are putting library news elsewhere in the library (near the circulation desk), you can devote this board to:

- Community news
- Personals (your decision).

While you cannot control the appearance of signs placed on the bulletin board, you can write up a short policy to cover the bulletin board:

- How long a notice can be left up;
- Notice must be signed
- May or may not be a commercial ad (real estate, hair dressers, massage parlors, and so on)
- Staff member must approve the posting
- Make the policy short enough to be placed on the board.

If you will be using a flat board to be hung on the wall, divide it into as many sections as you allow. This can be done with colored paper strips or tape. Place the title of each section at the top, clearly visible.

One library uses its left front window (the library is in a former storefront) as a bulletin board for all community events—no personals or commercial ads. The staff must constantly view this from outside to make sure it does not become cluttered and unsightly.

Another attractive style of bulletin board is the three- or four-sided kiosk type that is freestanding, placed where traffic goes around it and all four sides are easily viewed. It stands on legs or a base to place it at eye level, and should be tested for safety (and stability). Of course this style requires a little extra floor space, but if someone can build you one inexpensively, the information kiosk works beautifully and looks quite professional.

Whichever style you choose, keep it neat and do not leave outdated notices posted. Having one volunteer responsible for this is a good idea.

— PART THREE —
ESTABLISHING GOODWILL AND GOOD POLICIES

Chapter 14
A Climate for Development:
Ownership, Local Government,
Public Etiquette and Confidentiality

Chapter 15
Donations from the Community: Mixed Blessings

Chapter 16
Library Policies

Chapter 17
The Library Board: Policy and Bylaws

14

A Good Climate for Development: Ownership, Local Government, Public Etiquette and Confidentiality

Ownership of a Library

This is another of my pet subjects when talking about libraries. In most cases there are many supporters of a library: individuals, local governments, state libraries, federal agencies, corporations and businesses.

This kind of support creates the community's library. That is who it belongs to—not to any one member of the core group, not even to the group as a whole, not to any future director, but rather *to the community where it exists*. Remember: Any time you hear someone refer to the library as "our library," or "my library," you have my permission to roundly remind them: it is the *whole community's library*, and don't forget it!

If you have a donor who appears and supplies every nickel for its upkeep and collection, you will indeed have a private library that belongs to that donor. That donor can call it her or his library and make all the decisions.

Core groups cannot design a library with only their own tastes and preferences in mind. They need to reflect the whole community. That is why I suggested the core group be representative of the community, remember?

91

If you are secretly dreaming of a donor who will indeed offer to build what you want from the ground up and solve all your problems, listen to these two stories.

STORY ONE:

In a small village, the library was languishing and suffering in a damp, brick building with old wiring and no room for programs. Along came a wealthy benefactress who lavished money upon the library board and paid for the library to be reincarnated. It was moved to an historic railroad depot which received a new architecturally designed interior that was breathtaking and drew loud applause.

The benefactress then proceeded to place herself on the board and to drum the library director of 14 years right out the door. The Director disagreed with the benefactress's wishes as to collection development, when the Library should be open, and who could use the Internet. The other board members were reluctant to challenge the woman because they were afraid she would withdraw her financial support.

STORY TWO:

In another small town, surrounded by vineyards and artists' studios, a friend of mine was director of a tiny, attractive library situated smack on Main Street and filled with local art. Wiring was old and room to expand was nil. She had to pile catalogues and new books on the floor around her desk until she could get to them. Twenty-three children met for storytimes crammed into a small corner that had been adequate when only ten children attended years before.

One day a vineyard dowager came in to return her book and sat for a while chatting with my friend as she stamped books out, wrote interlibrary loan requests, directed patrons to areas they sought on the shelves, and tripped over those stacks on the floor.

"My," said the dowager, "you certainly could use more room here." And the next day her chauffeur arrived with a letter and the first of several checks for $50,000 to "help you get what you want."

My friend and her library board were able to create a wonderful library by buying the building next door, knocking out the wall between and meeting many needs of the community. Never once did the dowager come to criticize or suggest; she knew she had no library expertise and just shared an occasional visit with my friend to enjoy all the activity.

As I said, these two stories teach a lesson. There may or may not be hidden price tags when accepting that dream donation. Careful examination of a donor's motivation and intention are absolutely essential.

Wooing Your Local Government

Who do I mean by your local government? Here's who: mayor, village (or town) council, town clerk, municipal judges, school superintendent, municipal legal advisor, fire chief, water commissioner, and so forth. Do you know who is influential in your situation? (Please add any other position or community leader you can think of.)

What do I mean by "wooing?" No, I don't mean sending flowers or taking someone on a moonlight canoe ride. Rather, I mean simply talk to them. Let your mayor, town or village council know in basic terms that there is a group investigating the needs and necessities of starting a library, and that the group wants to keep them abreast of its progress.

Do this as you begin to meet and make plans. They will already know what you are doing anyway—the grapevine will see to that—so keep things open, friendly and informative, starting now. In all likelihood, the local government (at more than one level) will be approached sooner or later for financial support. If you start off on the proverbial right foot, things will go smoother and more naturally later.

If a council member or even the mayor is included in the core group, all the other government people should be informed; do not assume they will get the right news from other sources. Small towns are known for the grapevine; you want to avoid inaccurate rumors about a potential library getting out before your first meeting is over!

Another reason for being aboveboard is that remaining secretive about their meetings and plans may cause the core group to run the risk of being regarded as snobbish. "Their library" may be viewed as a private organization. Beware of this because it could haunt you later when you want to involve the community in funding or volunteering. I know in one case a library was thought to be "just Madeleine's pet project," not something affecting the whole community and eligible for local (public) funding.

Public Etiquette and Confidentiality

Public etiquette refers to how you as a group appear in the public eye. In public, the group should have as its trademark a united front; the community will see a professional and cooperative working team. (See Figure 1.1, Statement of Commitment.)

Disagreements happen, of course, (human beings are involved, after all!), and talking them through to consensus creates a stronger group. But be careful to air all library- and core group–related disagreements and gripes only within the core group meetings—not in the market, or post office or beauty parlor.

If there is a member who repeatedly airs core group disagreements outside meetings, a discussion on why such behavior is detrimental to the group's efforts should be held. Misunderstandings can be cleared up and the air cleared.

I recall when a committee member I was working with always had a gripe about how meetings were conducted. He never, however, talked about his dissatisfaction to the group. They would hear about his feelings around town at some of the places I mentioned already: the post office and hardware store. People treated the problem as a joke, but after a while began to think maybe those meetings really were not being done right and what was going on, anyway?

The member was reminded—by the very person who had asked him to serve—that he had agreed to work on a team. Teams couldn't accomplish much if one of the team's members was spreading bad and inaccurate news.

He tried to change his habits, but just could not keep from spreading word of things he didn't like abut the committee. He was asked to resign in favor of working on another committee of one—himself! Things went fine from then on—in both committees.

Remember, too, that one member of the group does not commit the core group to anything without the whole group discussing it first. This is especially important if someone tries to influence the planning ("I'll get you this if you'll do this other thing") or the potential collection ("You're not going to include those kinds of books in this library, are you? You won't see me there if you do!").

I remember being told by one very supportive woman that if "the state" got involved she was out of there with her support in her pocket. I replied by saying we had not reached the point of involving the state in anything yet—but I would give her plenty of warning. (It turned out she was talking about the state tax department, and I was talking about the state library!) She maintained her support.

15

Donations from
the Community:
Mixed Blessings

As soon as word gets out that the library board is really planning a library, donations of all kinds will start coming in. You will find they can be a mixed blessing. If you kept your list of potential supporter in-kind services (*see Worksheet 1.4, Appendix B*) you already know about some of the donations people are ready to give the library.

It will help the library board and all potential donors if you write a "Library Wish List" for donors and publicize it!

(*See Worksheet 15.1, Appendix B*.)

List what you really can use and need as "Excellent Donations":

- Up-to-date or new books, children's books in good condition
- Money
- New computers (or ones not more than two years old)
- Supplies appropriate for a library—paper clips, staplers, 3×5 cards, stamp pad and date stamp, notebooks, CLOSED/OPEN sign (see Chapter 19)
- Useful and appropriate furniture for a library—sturdy, clean (or cleanable)
- Adjustable shelving deep enough for large books
- Touch-tone telephone (that works)
- Card catalogue on its base (unless you are going right to computerized catalogue)

- Pens and pencils
- Paper for copiers, computers

There will also be unrequested—and not excellent—donations. What should you do when someone proudly comes in the door with one of these less-desirable items:

- Old college and high school text books
- 40 pounds of old *National Geographic* magazines without an Index
- 40 pounds of *Reader's Digest* magazines and condensed novels
- Old (partial-volume) magazines
- Books that are mildewed, coverless, chewed and otherwise distressed
- Rigid shelving units that do not fit larger books
- Old typewriters that "just need..."
- Obsolete computers or parts of computers not compatible with each other
- Answering machines, adding machines, etc., needing parts that cannot be bought anymore, or just plain do not work
- Pens and staplers that do not work, markers that are dried up, and so forth
- Television that does not work or cannot be connected to a VCR
- Dirty, wobbly (unsafe!) tables and upholstered furniture.

If you throw up your hands and say "Oh, we can't use that!" and refuse things, you may alienate donors. Instead, it's a good idea to be in a position to handle everything pleasantly, efficiently and quickly.

Here's how: write a "Policy for Donations." A policy done before a crisis arises can quite possibly keep confrontations and bad feelings from even beginning.

One purpose of policy is to explain what an organization does and does not do. It is created and used by the governing board, whatever form that may take. (That is why policies should be signed and dated.) Without a policy, someone can question, confront or intimidate a staff or board member and that member has no defined recourse to use as an answer.

A policy is both a protection for the library and the patron (or, in this case, the donor.) Both sides understand a situation as it is explained by the policy; there should be no surprises. A policy can be amended at any time as situations change.

Until you have a location for the library, find a dry storage place for all items as they are given—a shed or backroom would do—it does not have to be heated. Many times people will appear at the library door with things at inconvenient times for both board and staff. Remember, to them their donation is important and if they are told to come back at a more convenient time, you may never see them (as donors or patrons) again. Worse, they may tell others that you are not really interested in donations, or are "too good for my stuff."

Figure 15.1 provides a sample donation policy. You will see at the end it includes the date when it was adopted by the board.

Figure 15.1
SAMPLE DONATION POLICY

Handleberg Library Donation Policy
All items in good repair and useful to the Handleberg Library will be gratefully accepted. Since the Library is just being started, some items will be of more use right now than others. Receipts will be given when items are brought in person.

Books
All books must be clean and have covers. Children's books are a priority.

Old textbooks are not useful.

Furniture
Furniture should be clean and sturdy. It would help the Library Board if donors could check ahead of time to see if furniture will be of use right now.

Supplies & Equipment
Basic office supplies are accepted. Electronic equipment should be in working order and not obsolete

Money
Donations of money will go toward basic operating expenses unless designated by donor toward books or furnishings at time of donation.

Receipts for monetary donations will be given for amounts over $10.00.

Items not able to be used immediately will be stored and become the property of the Library if the donor does not want them back

This Policy Adopted by Handleberg Library Board of Trustees at its regular meeting, 6/5/97.

Believe me, even with a fine policy like this one, you will still get deliveries of items which are not clean, not in working order or just plain not useful.

I am reminded of the board member who arrived at the library one morning to find two old recliners sitting outside the door. It was almost impossible to get to the door; she had to find help to move them. Not only were they old, but they were cracked and dirty. Since they were not delivered in person by the "donor," the library board did not issue a receipt and felt justified in getting rid of them. The policy specifically said 1) donations of furniture had to be arranged beforehand, and 2) receipts were only given for donations made in person.

(See Worksheet 15.2, Appendix B.)

Unless a donation is particularly awful, it is in the best interest of community goodwill to smile and say "thank you." Should the person sincerely ask if you can use what he or she has, then be cheerfully honest and try to direct them somewhere the item will be of use. Have everyone fill out a donation receipt form, and somewhere in the form include the following statement shown in Figure 15.2 for them to sign and date:

Figure 15.2
EXERPT FROM DONATION RECEIPT FORM (15.3)

I understand that if the Library cannot use this (these) item(s), I will pick them up within one week of notification. After that, they become property of the Library.

Signature of donor _____   Date _____

A good donation receipt form covers who gave what, when they gave it, who received it, whether or not the donor wants the item(s) back and offers a receipt so the donor can assign value to the donation.

NOTE: Libraries are not to assign values to donations; they simply state that the item was given as a donation. No matter how many or how new the book(s), do not be forced into writing the value on the receipt.

Refer to Figure 15.3, Donation Receipt Form, for ideas.

(See Worksheet 15.3, Appendix B.)

Figure 15.3
SAMPLE DONATION RECEIPT FORM

DONATION RECEIPT FORM
Handleberg Library
Receipt and Record of Donation
Thank you for your donation to our Library!

Name _____

Address _____

_____

Telephone _____

continued on p. 99

---

continued from p. 98

DONATION RECEIPT FORM

Item (s)

Person accepting for Library _____   Date _____

I understand that if the Library cannot use this (these) item(s), I will pick them up
within one week of notification. After that, they become property of the Library.
Signature of donor _____   Date _____

Cut along line below and return to Donor

###

Received by _____, of Handleberg Library
Item(s) _____
_____
_____

From _____   Date _____

Donor will assign Value $_____

Thank you again for your contribution!
Handleberg Library Board Handleberg, YS

16

Library Policies

One purpose of policy within a library is to have an answer when disagreements or misunderstandings arise. Misunderstandings on the part of patrons, volunteers, board members and donors can be cleared up when a policy is in place to cover a potential crisis. Disagreements between board members, volunteers and patrons about how things should or should not have been done can be smoothed out by having policies read by all involved parties.

Misunderstandings and disagreements can occur in any of the following areas, and I suggest a Policy for each:

- Selection of materials
- Confidentiality
- Use of the facility by the community
- Appropriate library behavior
- Staff development
- Donations
- Reconsideration of library material (patron complaint about material)
- Fund-raising committees
- Internet use
- Borrowing/Loan
- Library board
- Volunteers
- Juvenile volunteers

Basically, a policy should state the way the library wants things done, whether it is selecting materials, "hiring" volunteers, loaning materials, letting community groups use the library, and so forth.

The board sets policy, with advice and input from the director. A policy is a friend to those who care about a library and want it to work with as few upsetting incidents as possible.

The best advice I can give about policy is to consider as many situations as you can ahead of any unexpected crisis. Crises do occur, and to be prepared with a policy composed in calmer times will be a big help.

Posting some policies is a good idea, too. Policies on confidentiality, borrowing/loan, Internet use, and the appropriate library behavior are all good ones to have in plain view. All policies, however, should be kept in a notebook where all patrons and staff can read them at any time. Policies are not secrets; they help things to run more smoothly over bumpy roads.

I have already included several examples of good policy in this book: one dealing with donations , another on board policy and one dealing with confidentiality. There are more examples at the end of the chapter in Figures 16.1 through 16.8. You may borrow from any of these, modifying them to your needs and community.

Policies can be changed, and should be examined from year to year to see if they are still pertinent to the community and the library they are designed to help. Changes should be made to better serve the library, not a member of the Board or someone in the community.

I had a little trouble once with some board members who thought they could do as they pleased when it came to paying fines, adhering to loan periods and using the building. It was a struggle to get them to see that not only were they ignoring policy, but they were setting a bad example to the community. If board members do not follow policy, why should other people?

Figure 16.1
SAMPLE MATERIALS SELECTION POLICY

HANDLEBERG LIBRARY
SELECTION POLICY

I. Responsibility for Materials Selection

Final responsibility for selection of all materials rests with the Library Board, upon the recommendation of the Library Director, and under the guidelines of this policy.

II. Principles of Selection

1. Popular demand: repeated requests for titles, author, and/or subject areas
2. Timeliness and accuracy
3. Balance within the subject area
4. Cost in consideration of entire book budget
5. Reviews and recommendations
6. School-recommended titles and subjects areas
7. Physical condition in cases of donated materials

III. Scope of the Collection in Order of Importance

1. Recreational reading for children and adults
2. Reference collection (for in-library use only)
3. Basic, balanced nonfiction collection
4. A Southwest collection reflective as possible of the region
5. Audio books for adults and children
6. Collections reflective of community needs:
   - large-print titles in fiction and nonfiction
   - family-centered "Books & Us"
   - Bound for Home—book bags to homebound patrons

IV. Relevancy to the Community and Goals of the Library

Handleberg Library emphasizes recreational reading at all age levels.

The nonfiction collection will reflect the interests and needs of the service area. The basic reference collection will include dictionaries, almanacs, local directories, useful state publications, county and state rosters, local telephone books, and a current one-volume desk encyclopedia. At least one set of encyclopedias will be available.

V. Donations, Memorial Books, and Gifts

See *Donations Policy*.

VI. Weeding

All collections need regular examination to remove titles no longer appropriate, accurate or useful. This will make room for new titles and will keep the library from becoming cluttered.

Principles of Selection for Elimination from the Collection

1. Bad physical condition
2. Defacement by patron use
3. No longer timely and accurate: may be harmful or dangerous
4. Unbalance within the subject area
5. More than a year since last circulation
6. Need for shelf space.

continued on page 104

(continued from page 103)

VII. Recommendations by Patrons

Recommendations by patrons will be considered in conjunction with this policy.

VIII. Removal of Items from Collection by Patron Request

See *Patron Request for Reconsideration of Library Materials* form and policy.

Approved for submission to State Library at regular Library Board meeting, April 1999.

Figure 16.2
SAMPLE RECONSIDERATION OF MATERIAL POLICY

HANDLEBERG LIBRARY
RECONSIDERATION OF MATERIAL POLICY

When a patron objects to material found in Handleberg Library, the following policy will aid patron and Library Board in resolving the matter.

1. Objections to any Library material must be made, on the *Patron Request for Reconsideration of Library Materials* Form provided by the Library.
2. The Library Board or Director will not consider verbal objections or complaints made on other paper.
3. The form must be signed by the patron making the complaint.
4. The Library Director will present the reconsideration form, the material concerned, reviews of the material (when possible), the *ALA Library Bill of Rights*, and this selection policy to the Library Board at its next regular meeting.
5. The Board will try to resolve the matter at that meeting, or will schedule a special meeting for that purpose.
6. If a special meeting is needed, the patron will be notified as soon as possible and may be asked to attend.
7. A letter of decision will be sent from the Board to the patron who initiated the request for reconsideration.

Approval Date April 1999

Figure 16.3
SAMPLE FORM FOR PATRON RECONSIDERATION REQUEST

HANDLEBERG LIBRARY
PATRON REQUEST FOR RECONSIDERATION
OF LIBRARY MATERIALS

To: Handleberg Library Board of Trustees   Date: _____

From:

Patron's full name: ————————————————————————————

Address: ————————————————————————————————

Town: _____ Zip: _____ Telephone _____

Material being proposed for reconsideration:

Title: _____

Author: _____

Call number: _____ Date of pub. _____

Why are you concerned about this material and on what are you basing this concern?

Have you read the entire book?

Please list exact pages that you are concerned about, and why.

Do you know of another unobjectionable book you could recommend on the same subject?

Title:_____ Author: _____

Publisher:_____ Why do you prefer this book?

_____

Thank you for answering these questions. We are always glad to have patrons express their views and interests in the Library. Your concern will be brought to the Library Board at its next regular meeting, discussed in light of Handleberg Library's Selection Policy, and a resolution will be sought in a timely manner. A response will be sent to you as soon as possible. In the meantime, we hope you will continue to come and use the Library.

Figure 16.4
SAMPLE BORROWING/LOAN POLICY

HANDLEBERG LIBRARY
BORROWING/ LOAN OF MATERIALS POLICY

I. Who may borrow materials

Anyone having a telephone and a *physical* address in Handleburg, in Your County, or in Your State, where they can be contacted may borrow materials from Handleberg Library.

   1. Out-of-state borrowers must list state driver's license number on registration card.

   2. While all Your State library cards—public, academic and public school libraries—will be honored, potential borrowers must register in the above manner.

II. Registration and Library Cards

  A. Registration is free; a card will be given with a sequential number.

   1. Prior to age eight it is necessary for children to use parent's or guardian's card, or have parent or guardian sign jointly with the child on the child's card to hold joint responsibility of materials borrowed.

   2. At age eight, patrons are eligible for their own Library card.

   3. The patron's number, not the patron's name, will be used to sign out materials. This protects the patron's privacy.

III. Fines, Fees and Charges

There will be a charge for lost Library cards of $0.25 (twenty-five cents).

There will be a charge for lost or materials damaged beyond further use to the Library. The charge will be the cost of the item plus $1.00 (one dollar) for processing.

Extended use fees for patrons:

   1. Rationale for changing extended use fees

The Handleberg Library Board understands that its circulating items are of interest to more than one patron. If articles are returned on time or renewed in a timely manner, they will be available to all patrons. The items owned by the Library, whether they have been selected from donations or purchased, are all important to the collection.

   2. Definition of an overdue article

Articles kept beyond the last day of the loan period indicated on article pocket or date slip shall be considered in extended use, and so shall be assigned a fee.

3. Extended use period defined

Duration of an extended use fee will commence the first day of overdue status and will run up to the day before the patron comes in to pay.

Example: If the article is due on the eighteenth and the person comes in with it on the nineteenth, the nineteenth will not be included in the fee.

4. Renewing materials

Renewals may be made prior to or on the actual due date. They may be done by telephone with the patron understanding that it is their responsibility to note the change in due date on the article they have in hand.

5. Extended borrowing periods

Long-term borrowing periods may be arranged in special circumstances such as homeschool needs, special assignments or vacation travel.

6. Notification of overdue materials

The person to whom the article is checked out will receive a card indicating the above condition. Cards will be sent once a month, and a record of each sending will be attached to the overdue articles card.

7. Amount of extended use fee:

• An extended use fee of $0.10 (ten cents) per day per article will be charged, for adult and juvenile books, and magazines. Days the Library is closed will not be counted.

• An extended use fee of $0.50 (fifty cents) per day per video and audio article will be charged.

• All extended use fees will be capped in the following manner:

Hardbound articles will accumulate a fee no greater than $5.00.

Paperbound articles will accumulate a fee no greater than $3.00.

Audio and video articles will accumulate a fee no greater than $5.00.

8. All extended use fees will be put toward the purchase of new Library circulating materials and thus can be considered a contribution or donation to the Library.

IV. Responsibility for choosing and borrowing materials

The choice of what to borrow rests with the borrower, and is not the responsibility of Library staff.

V. Responsibility and care of borrowed materials

Responsibility and care of borrowed materials rests with the patron; there will be a charge for lost and severely damaged materials.

(continued on page 108)

(continued from page 107)

VI. Loan Period

There is a loan period of two weeks for all materials unless otherwise arranged at time of checkout.

    1. Return of materials may be during Open Hours or in the Book Drop

    2. Patrons will be reminded that all Library materials may be needed by others; prompt return is expected.

Figure 16.5
EXAMPLE FACILITY USAGE POLICY

HANDLEBERG LIBRARY
FACILITY POLICY

While it is not part of the mission of the Handleberg Library to provide meeting space for community organizations, in keeping with the American Library Association's *Library Bill of Rights*, the Handleberg Library facility is available to non-profit organizations serving the Handleberg community on a reservation basis for cultural, educational or civic purposes.

I. Responsibility for Determining Use of Facility

Requests for facility use must be taken to the whole Board at a regular or special Library Board meeting. Neither a Board member on his/her own, nor the Director, nor any staff member may give permission for use of the facility by any group. The following considerations will help the Library Board in their decision.

II. Priorities for Use of the Meeting Rooms

    1. Library-sponsored meetings or programs

    2. Library-related meetings or programs

    3. Meetings sponsored by agencies of the town of Handleberg

    4. Educational, cultural or civic meetings, or programs of organizations

    5. Other meetings which in the opinion of the Library Board are appropriate to the Library.

Examples: literacy tutoring, book discussion groups, children's programming, parenting groups, homeschooling programs, nature talks, artists' seminars, author talks, cultural talks, and others as determined by the Board.

III. Restrictions

  1. The Board will refuse use of the facility to any group who discriminates attendance at the meetings by race, sex, cultural origin or other methods.
  2. In compliance with the Fire Marshal, no more than ____ people may use the facility at one time.
  3. No conduct disturbing regular library use or infringing on any library rules is permitted.
  4. There is NO SMOKING in the Library facility or in the restroom. There will be no open flames (candles, incense, etc.)
  5. Any arts and crafts activities will not involve Library furniture or supplies.
  6. Nothing can be affixed to the walls.
  7. There will no religious services, cooking, or physical activities.
  8. No alcoholic beverages are permitted on the premises.
       Food or beverages may not be served except at specially designated Library events.
  9. The use of the meeting rooms may not interfere with normal operation of the Library.
       Meetings may be held in Library meeting rooms between the following hours on days the Library is open. (List days and hours.) Arrangements must be made for using the Library during closed hours.
       The Library reserves the right to change a scheduled meeting date which conflicts with the Library operation.
  10. The Library accepts no responsibility for any meeting-related expenses.
       Publicity is the responsibility of groups booking meeting rooms. Groups must provide and produce their own publicity. Groups must be identified on all publicity as sponsoring the meeting. Publicity may not imply that the Handleberg Library is in any manner connected with the meeting except for providing meeting space.
  11. Except for the Friends of the Library, organizations meeting in the Library may not use the Library as a mailing address, or the Library telephone number to conduct their business.
  12. Keys to the building are not available to user groups.

IV. Fees and Charges

No charge is made for the use of the meeting room and no admission fee may be charged or donations collected in the Library for programs presented.
  Donations toward the maintenance of the facility will be accepted.

V. Responsibilities

Library Board

(continued on page 110)

(continued from page 109)

1. Release from liability: The library is not responsible for accidents, injury, loss or damage to the private property of individuals or organizations. The Library Board and staff will not be responsible for the property of individuals or organizations meeting in the library or for storage of materials.
2. A trustee or staff member will be present in the Library during all meetings.

Party Requesting Use of Facility

1. Exact dates and times will be available to Library Board for Consideration. There will be no acceptance of casual or inexact schedules.
2. Meeting room users may not offer items or services for sale while on library premises, solicit orders for goods or services, or engage in other fund-raising activities.
3. One person from the group will be responsible for:
   - Reading and making group aware of this policy, and in particular, the above restrictions
   - Being personally present at each meeting
   - Damages incurred during the meetings. Damage incurred to library property will be the responsibility of the person or group reserving the meeting room, and costs will be billed accordingly. If more than routine cleaning is necessary the person or group will be billed accordingly.
   - Rearrangement of furniture
   - Removal of any items pertaining to group.
4. This person will sign a Library Facility Use Contract. (*attached*)
5. No group or organization may reassign use of the facilities to another.
6. Groups of persons under 18 years of age must be accompanied by a responsible adult.

VI. Continuation or Termination of Facility Use

1. Groups may continue to use facility as long as no deviation from the Contract occurs.
2. If the Board determines a deviation has occurred, they have the right to terminate the Contract immediately and may refuse further use of the facility to that particular group.
3. If the group wishes to terminate its meetings earlier than stated in the contract, that will be acceptable to the Board.
4. If the group wishes to renew or extend a contract, it must again have approval of entire Library Board. (See Section I.)

Amendments to this Policy may be made at any time with entire Board approval.
Approval Date April 1999

Figure 16.6
EXAMPLE STAFF DEVELOPMENT POLICY

HANDLEBERG LIBRARY
STAFF DEVELOPMENT POLICY—*May 1999*

To develop and maintain a dynamic and dedicated staff—including Director, staff and volunteer group—it is necessary to provide opportunities for further education and individual improvement within the library field.

I. Role of the Library Board in Staff Development

   A. It is the job of the Library Board to select the best Director possible for Handleberg Library.

   B. When no degree in library science exists, the Board should stipulate that the Director become Grade II certified by the State Library at the first opportunity. The Board should try to cover any hardship costs.

   C. The Board should support the Director in recruiting able and committed people to help cover advertised operating hours.

   D. The Board should fund (by seeking funding sources):
   • Attendance by Director at Your State Library Association conferences and workshops .
   • Subscription to one or two professional journals to help the Director keep abreast of Library developments.

   E. The Board should create a method of evaluating the Director on an annual basis. [*See* Attachment I: Job Description of the Library Director, following Section III of this policy.]

II. Development of the Director

   A. At the first opportunity, the Director will achieve certification by the State Library unless he or she already holds an MLS.

   B. The Director will join Your State Library Association and annually attend its conference.

   C. The Director should take advantage of the State Library support staff, and State Library books and periodicals

   D. The Director will receive and read the weekly newsletter from the State Library.

III. Development of the Library Staff

   A. The primary source for in-house staff development is the Director, who:
   • Fosters an overall awareness of librarianship when appropriate (staff members will see how small tasks affect the whole organization)

(continued on page 112)

(continued from page 111)

- Designates tasks and duties to all staff members based on their knowledge and skills already in place
- Fosters a desire to gain new knowledge and learn new skills
- Encourages staff to attend workshops and conferences
- Shares articles from library literature and posts staff notes on a bulletin board
- Schedules monthly staff meetings involving concerns and questions of the staff, concerns of the Director, a specific area of the Library or Library's collection, news from libraries elsewhere.
- Encourages staff questions and suggestions at any time
- Makes time to work alongside staff members to take note of their performances and to suggest better methods of performance
- Creates and updates procedure manual for all staff
- Requires reading of all Library policies
- Evaluates staff members on an annual basis.

B. Available External Development Opportunity Sources

- The Director will encourage all staff members to study and take the exams for Your State Grade I / II state certification when offered.
- All staff members should join the Your State Library Association.
- The weekly newsletter and the quarterly Your State Library Association newsletter should be available to all staff.
- They should be encouraged to attend the Your State Library Association conferences for lectures and to see library products.
- Attendance at Your State Library workshops should be encouraged.
- Visits to other libraries should be encouraged.
- When financially possible, at least one subscription to a professional journal should be purchased for the staff and pertinent articles read by all staff.

Attachment I

Job Decription of Library Director

Responsibilities of the Director include, but are not limited to:
Day-to-day running of the library.
Creating (and abiding by) all library policies and procedures.
Selection/dismissal of all staff.
Selection of materials according to a selection policy.
Assigning jobs to staff (volunteer or paid) and readjusting or expanding those jobs when necessary.

Training staff through workshops and monthly staff meetings.

Report to the library board at monthly meetings.

Suggesting to Board needed changes, additions, improvements to library.

Representing library at community meetings or selecting someone to do so.

Qualifications

Education:

Must have completed a college degree; MLS degree would be ideal.

Degree should have included literature courses.

A "reading background."

Experience:

Documented* experience as a supervisor in a situation comparable to (if not in) a library setting.

Public service–oriented work experience: must be a "people person" desiring to help people of all types and backgrounds.

Must be able to work with volunteers for the benefit of the library.

Must be able to make decisions quickly as well as thoughtfully.

Skills and Knowledge:

If MLS is not present, must demonstrate understanding of "what a Library is all about" (its role, its purpose).

Must have documented* organizational and recordkeeping skills.

Must be able to create policies, handouts, schedules, reports; should be familiar with grant-writing.

Should establish an atmosphere of challenge and excitement within library environment; must be able to direct others in a helpful, firm and positive manner.

Approved for submission to State Library at regular Board Meeting June 1999

Make sure an applicant has actual references or documentation; verbal assurances alone should not be accepted.

Figure 16.7
SAMPLE DONATIONS POLICY

HANDLEBERG LIBRARY
DONATIONS POLICY

I. BOOKS

The Handleberg Library accepts donations of books, by single copies and in bulk amounts. The staff will make every effort to incorporate donated titles into the collection, using the Selection Policy in this manual.

A. Receiving and Leaving Book Donations

1. The Library urges donations of books be left when the Library is open; some volunteers cannot lift heavy boxes. (When the weather is unpredictable, donations may be damaged.)

2. If the Library is closed, the donor is urged to call the telephone number(s) left by the door; arrangements can be made for delivery or pickup.

3. Books left outside the door cannot be receipted.

4. Books left anonymously automatically become the property of the Library, to do with as it sees fit.

B. Selecting Books from Donations

Using the Selection Policy as a guide, all donated books will be considered for their usefulness and appropriateness to the whole collection. Handleberg Library will make every effort to incorporate donated books into its collection. There are, however, times when this is not possible.

1. Some reasons for not keeping a donated book may be:

   • Condition

   • Duplication of title or subject matter

   • Age (accuracy and currentness of material)

   • "Not wanted" list—
     business and school (and college) textbooks more than a year old
     *National Geographic*s issues unless accompanied by an index,
       Reader's Digest and condensed volumes
     (When possible, any of these will be returned to the donor at the time of donation.)

2. Books not useful to collection:
   Handleberg Library will donate or sell or otherwise dispose of books not useful to the collection. If the donor wants them back, this should be determined when the donation is left. See D. 1.

3. A free magazine and newspaper table will be established. Donated magazines will be placed on this table. Magazines may be read or swapped.

C. Memorial Books and Special Collections
  1. Memorial books:
      - Suggestions for memorial book titles or subject areas can be made by the Director.
      - The book then can be purchased by either the patron, or by the Director, upon receipt of the amount needed for purchase.
      - Memorial books can be given for any age group.
      - A bookplate will be placed in the book, mentioning the person donating the book, the date, and the person's name in whose memory it was given.
  2. Special Collections:
      A private, special collection—a group of books sharing a theme or author—may be of use and value to the Library collection.

      Such collections will be considered by the Director, using the Library Mission Statement and Selection Policy as guides.

      Such collections—if placed on the shelf as circulating or reference material—will have a bookplate placed in each volume with the donor's name and date of donation.

D. Receipts; Recognition of Book Donations
  1. During Open Hours, all book donations can be "receipted" in general terms at time of donation, using the official form.
  2. Values of books cannot be given. Instead, "two boxes of books" or "five books" or " a collection of sixteen books on Mexican history" will be listed.
  3. A record of all book donations (in general terms) will be kept in the Library, listed by date and donor.
  4. Thank-you notes will be written for all books given; it shall be one Board member's responsibility to do so, and it shall be at the discretion of that Board member to mention bulk gifts, specific titles, memorials, and so forth.
  5. Periodically, all donations given to the Library will be mentioned in the newspaper.

Approved at regular Board meeting on _____
      Signed, _____President

Figure 16.8
EXAMPLE FUND-RAISING EVENTS POLICY

HANDLEBERG LIBRARY
FUND-RAISING EVENTS POLICY

I. The chairman of each event shall determine the following, as applicable:
  • Time of sales and entrance to the event (i.e., early sales, saved items)
  • Pricing decisions (tickets, items sold, reducing prices)
  • When donations to event will be accepted
  • All arrangements for guest demonstrators and speakers, arrival and set-up time, equipment, supplies

II. While a chairman delegates responsibility for various aspects of the project to committee members, all *final* responsibility for events rests with the chairman.

III. Each chairman will:
  • Report to the entire Board when asked to do so by the president.
  • Ask all who worked on a project to fill out and return an evaluation form; the chairman may compile those evaluations, or give them to the fund-raising chairman.

17

The Library Board:
Policy and Bylaws

I think the core group can become or elect the library board of trustees once the basic jobs have been accomplished: the timeline, the community assessment, and the community list at least begun. These topics are covered in their own chapters.

A Library board of trustees is responsible for the library's fiscal and physical well-being. The board will then write a set of bylaws (or board policy) that detail the makeup of the board, duties and responsibilities involved, and when and how it meets.

It is my intention here to keep coverage of these subjects as simple as possible; there is plenty of information out there specifically on library boards and board bylaws. I mainly want to spend my time on other aspects of the library.

The Library Board of Trustees

A library board can have as few as five to as many members as the group wishes. Remember, though, a quorum (a majority plus one) must be present at a meeting in order to conduct business, so the fewer the members, the lower the quorum needed. Your group may decide to nominate all officers of the board from the core group with any remaining group members being members-at-large.

A board traditionally includes a president, vice-president, recording secretary, treasurer and members-at-large. Duties generally include:

- President—someone who is respected in the community, who can keep pleasant control of a meeting and completes tasks.
- Vice-President—can serve in the president's absence.
- Recording Secretary—someone who takes thorough, unbiased minutes, corresponds well, and can keep track of all important papers.
- Treasurer—a person respected in the community who has knowledge of financial record-keeping.
- Members-at-large—may vote and take part in all projects and duties.

DIFFERENCE BETWEEN DUTIES OF THE BOARD AND THE THOSE OF DIRECTOR

Even if someone from the core group or the library board ultimately serves as the library director, there is an important distinction to make between that job and the board's. Indeed, the director cannot serve on the board. If these two roles become confused, the library can suffer due to friction. Many times directors (librarians) do things a board should be doing, and vice versa.

The director is responsible for the day-to-day running of the library. Board members are responsible for the facility empowering the director, and by acting on the director's suggestions and concerns.

I once knew a board president whose director never opened her mouth at meetings. The board president disregarded her reports and suggestions, interfered with staff, fiddled with computer program installations, purchased and installed library shelving that was inadequate to needs, and in general gave everyone a headache at library board meetings. Meanwhile, the roof leaked, the children's section was dim and badly needed a coat of paint, there was no fund-raising activity taking place, and the front steps were not handicapped accessible.

The following table in Figure 17.1 shows which shoes should have been on whose feet!

Figure 17.1
EXAMPLE JOB DIFFERENCES: BOARD/DIRECTOR

JOB DESCRIPTIONS

BOARD	DIRECTOR (PART-TIME, OR FULL-TIME)
Facility (building, utilities, problems)	Selection of materials; plans programs, expands services as money and time allow
All financial responsibilities; keeps books and bank business	Petty cash; takes in whatever passes through library day-to-day. Can have checking account for purchases (book orders, subscriptions, supplies)
Can pay for book orders, subscriptions, supplies	
Fund-raising plan, staffing events	Suggests fund-raising needs and ideas.
Hires director	Hires staff; volunteers
Decides policies on recommendation of director	Suggests policy changes and needs to board
Sets agenda for monthly meetings with input from director; takes detailed minutes at each meeting and includes director's report	Attends monthly meetings; makes additions to agenda; makes a monthly report
Plans and sets goals for library in consultation with director	Works on plan with board
Represents library within community; is involved in community(ties); tries to form partnerships ($$)	Represents library within community; is involved with community(ties); tries to see cooperative possibilities

---

While this is a mouthful, it makes plain, I hope, the difference in the two roles. There are, as I have shown, jobs that either one, the other or both together can do. (This may be a handy list to remember for future reference.)

Library Bylaws and Board Policy

Library bylaws (or library board policy) describe why the library exists, and the who, when and how of the library board's makeup and duties. They tell what an agenda should cover at board meetings, what committees to consider, how to get second-rate (progress impeding, regularly absent) board members off the board and other useful things.

I have included a full board policy in Figure 17.2; you may modify or simplify it, although all articles are important. You may adopt this board policy as your own, changing names, dates, and so on, as necessary.

If you have someone in the legal field in your group—or on the potential board—that is a plus for you; have that person examine your board policy to make sure it covers what is necessary.

Figure 17.2
Sample Bylaws or Board Policy

Handleberg Library
Bylaws or Board Policy

ARTICLE I
MISSION STATEMENT

The Handleberg Library offers recreational and basic informational materials and services to the town of Handleberg.

It seeks to serve the town through community assessment, reevaluation of its services and collection, and by cooperative efforts with the nearby educational institutions.

In a broader sense, it is available to any and all neighboring areas, and honors other Your State library cards; it seeks to serve all borrowers in the best way possible.

Handleberg Library joins the libraries within Your State to offer and improve services to all who seek them.

ARTICLE II
BOARD SIZE, ROLE OF MEMBERS
AND DURATION OF TERM OF SERVICE

SECTION ONE: SIZE OF BOARD OF TRUSTEES

A. The Handleberg Library shall be governed by a Board of Trustees (henceforth to be known as "the Board") containing no fewer than 5 and no more than 7 members.

B. In its administrative and advisory capacity over the Library, the Board shall have the general control and management thereof, including the following powers and duties:

---

1. Public Support—Through the Friends of Handleberg Library, to seek and receive gifts, bequests, donations, grants or other gifts of all kinds for the support, maintenance and development of the Library and its collections, materials, buildings and equipment.

2. Annual Operating Budget—To provide an annual operating Library budget, in proper format. The budget covering the general operation of the Library, when adopted, shall be binding upon the Board and no expense may be made except in compliance with the approved budget. Provided, however, that if the Board determines that certain budgetary changes are necessary they may be properly submitted to the entire Board for approval.

3. Bylaws, Rules and Regulations—To make bylaws, policies and rules for the proper operation and use of the Library, which shall not be in conflict with any ordinances of the town of Handleberg or with the laws of the state of _____. One copy of such bylaws, rules and regulations adopted by the Board regulating the operation and use of the Library shall be filed with the Town Council and another copy shall be posted in a conspicuous place in the library.

4. Selection of Library Director and Other Personnel—To establish qualifications and responsibilities of a Director, subject to Article VIII hereof, and other library personnel and volunteers; advertise for and screen applicants; hire Director.

5. Reports to Town Council and Requests for Action—To make such reports as may be necessary to the Council as to the activities of the Board and Library and to request from the Handleberg Town Council any actions deemed necessary for the maintenance of the Library's collections, materials, buildings or equipment.

6. Long-range Planning—To establish long-range planning procedures and a course for the future development of the Library covering activities such as:
    a. Coordination of the activities of the Library with those of the Mayor and Town Council, civic groups, and other community organizations.
    b. Conducting community assessment programs to aid the Library in the efficient serving of the particular needs of the community served.
    c. Awareness of local, state and federal laws relating to the operation of the Library and to support legislation which improves and extends library services to all the members of the community.
    d. Development of sources of support through the statewide library development program, develop a working relationship with Your State Library System and develop cooperative efforts with other regional and county library systems.

(continued on page 122)

(continued from page 121)

    e. Providing for the development of the knowledge of library standards and trends by establishing training programs for the Board and Library personnel.

SECTION THREE: TERM OF SERVICE, VACANCIES AND REMOVALS

A. The members of the Board shall hold terms of three years. A member may serve two and only two consecutive three-year membership terms.
B. Members of the Board absent from three consecutive meetings without prior or sufficient notification shall be considered to have resigned, and will be asked to submit a letter to that effect.
C. As vacancies occur in the composition of the Board, they shall be filled with representatives of the Library's service area as suggested by the remaining Board members.
D. A list of potential Board members, from which vacancies can be filled, will be kept by the President.
E. Members of the Board may be removed from office only on the grounds of just and sufficient cause, with a vote taken by two-thirds of the membership of the Board.

ARTICLE III
OFFICERS OF THE BOARD OF TRUSTEES
AND THEIR ELECTION

SECTION ONE: OFFICERS

A. The members shall select from among their group a President, Vice-President, Recording Secretary and Treasurer, and such other officers as may be deemed necessary by the Board to carry out the functions of the Board. The offices of Secretary and Treasurer may be held by one person. Each officer shall serve for a term of one year and may hold consecutive terms in the office.
B. Board members other than officers will be Members-at-Large and will accept duties as assigned by the President.

SECTION TWO: ELECTION OF OFFICERS

A. Nominations of officers will be made at the regular monthly meeting one month prior to the annual meeting.
B. The officers shall be voted on at the commencement of the annual meeting and will begin their offices at the commencement of the new fiscal year.

ARTICLE IV
DUTIES OF OFFICERS

Section One: President.   The President shall be the presiding officer at all regular meetings, shall call special meetings as necessary, shall employ correct parliamentary proceedings, shall appoint standing committee chairmen and other committees as needed, will prepare an agenda for each meeting, and shall sign all official papers.

Section Two: Vice-President.   The Vice-President shall have all powers of the President in the event of the President's absence or refusal to act; the Vice-President will monitor and coordinate all working committees, and will report to the President and at all meetings on such.

Section Three: Recording Secretary.   The Recording Secretary will attend and will record in orderly fashion the minutes of each meeting convened by the President. These minutes will be maintained in a central location and shall be available to the public at any time.
   A. A copy of the Director's monthly report will be kept as part of the minutes.
   B. All communications made to and by the Library will be housed in this notebook.
   C. A record of all policies and procedures passed by the Board will be kept in a second notebook which will also be available to the public.
   D. The Recording Secretary shall post notices of all regular and special meetings in accordance with the open meeting law.

Section Four: Treasurer.   The Treasurer will collect and deposit all monies earned by and contributed to the Library, and will use a bank of the Board's designation. The Treasurer shall keep a record of all financial transactions, and will report on such transactions to the Board at each monthly meeting.
   A. The Treasurer shall pay all bills in a timely manner and will immediately alert the Board of any problems.
   B. A financial report and viewing of all transactions can be asked for at any time by any member of the Board; such a request should be put on the agenda prior to the regular meeting.
   C. The treasurer shall prepare an annual report for presentation at the annual meeting, and shall be responsible for preparing and mailing of all tax returns in a timely manner as required by state and federal tax agencies.

(continued on page 124)

(continued from page 123)

ARTICLE V
FISCAL YEAR

The fiscal year of Handleberg Library shall begin on January 1 and end on December 31.

ARTICLE VI
MEETINGS AND ORDER OF BUSINESS

SECTION ONE: REGULAR MONTHLY MEETINGS

The Board shall hold regular monthly meetings at a time and place to be fixed by the Board at its first meeting of the fiscal year. During the first meeting of the Board it will also adopt rules governing its proceedings. A copy shall be posted in a conspicuous place in the Library. The time and place of meeting may be changed by the Board by motion duly adopted at a regular or special meeting. A quorum of the Board shall be necessary for the transaction of business and the quorum number shall be fixed at the first meeting of the Board, all members attending.

SECTION TWO: SPECIAL MEETINGS AND EXECUTIVE SESSIONS

Special meetings and executive sessions may be called by the President or any member of the Board to deal with issues. A quorum of the Board shall be necessary for the transaction of business at any special meeting or executive session. Personnel issues will only be conducted in executive session.

SECTION THREE: ORDER OF BUSINESS

All regular monthly meetings shall be conducted according to *Robert's Rules of Order* and shall contain the following:
A.   Call to order
B.   Minutes from previous meeting
C.   Treasurer's report
D.   Director's report
E.   Committee Chairmen's reports
F.   Old business (unfinished)
G.   New business
H.   Election of officers at annual meeting
I.   Appointment of Committees (at first regular meeting only)

(continued on page 125)

J.   Setting of next meeting date

K.   Adjournment

[Do not worry about Articles VII and VIII at this time. You can examine them later as needed; for now skip to Article IX.]

ARTICLE VII
STANDING COMMITTEES AND CHAIRMEN'S DUTIES

SECTION ONE: STANDING COMMITTEES

The Standing Committees of the Handleberg Library shall be:

A.   Volunteer Committee (the Coordinator)

B.   Nominating Committee

C.   Budget Committee

D.   Planning Committee

E.   Fund-raising Committee.

SECTION TWO: COMMITTEE FORMATION

A.   Standing Committees shall be listed by the President at the first regular meeting of the year. Any Board member may volunteer to Chair a committee, or Chairmen will be appointed by the President. At the discretion of the President, a Chairman may be appointed from the community at large.

B.   These committees shall have one Board member serve as temporary Chairman. It will be the responsibility of this Chairman to develop a workable committee composed of patrons and interested people within the service area. A new, permanent Chairman can be chosen by this group if it so desires.

SECTION THREE: DUTIES OF COMMITTEE CHAIRMEN

A.   The Board President will ask for reports from the Committee Chairmen in a timely manner.

B.   It is the duty of the Committee Chairmen to promptly begin work and make reports to the Board at regular or special meetings.

ARTICLE VIII
LIBRARY DIRECTOR

A.   The operation of the Library shall be under the charge of a professional Library Director or a certified Library Technician in accordance with Your State Library System requirements, and shall be hired by the Board pursuant

(continued on page 126)

(continued from page 125)

to Article II, Section Two, B.4. The Director will report on the activities of the Library to the Board at its monthly meeting. The Director will be responsible for the selection and acquisition of materials for circulation, and for the acquisition of supplies and equipment, building renovations and the like.

B. The Director will be responsible for the daily operation of the Library and for the overseeing of Library staff.

C. A current job description of the Director/Technician position will be kept on file.

D. An evaluation of this position will be conducted annually, or at a time to be decided by the Board, based on time of hire.

ARTICLE IX
AMENDMENTS TO THE BYLAWS

A. Amendments may be made to the Bylaws in accordance with Your State Library requirements.

B. Amendments will require a two-thirds majority vote at a duly noted meeting with the full Board present.

C. All members will sign each amendment as it is made.

Notice how each Article is devoted to one important area; the areas flow from one area into the next related area.

Make sure each and every Board Member signs and dates this policy when it is passed.

— PART FOUR —
SUPPLIES, STAFF AND CIRCULATING MATERIALS

18

Supplies and Suppliers

Having the supplies you need for the daily library procedures is important. Use seed money for these or find a donor who will help you buy the first batch. If you have the necessary supplies when you need them, procedures can be carried out smoothly, and there will not be that frantic running around which frustrates and sometimes embarrasses staff and board alike.

There are basic office supplies I think every library needs. You may receive some as donations, new or used, but others you will want to purchase brand new. I list these in Figure 18.1.

Figure 18.1
Basic Supplies

Library stamp	current telephone	colored paper	paper towels
scotch tape	book	markers	broom
paper clips	calendar	library supply cat-	pads of lined
stapler (with sta-	3 × 5 unruled or	alogue	paper
ples that fit)	ruled cards	thumb tacks	work table—tem-
rubber bands	file drawers	light bulbs	porary or
pencils with	boxes to fit 3 × 5	cleaning supplies	permanent—
erasers	cards	for bathroom	washable and
pens	library registra-	good vacuum	sturdy enough
3-hole notebook	tion cards	with extra	for piles of
for statistics	note pads	bags	books
touch-tone tele-	rubber cement	dust cloths	
phone	glue	window cleaner	

Set the things you will use every day on the desk, ready to use. Store the other supplies neatly so when you reach for them, they are not buried in a drawer somewhere.

Book processing supplies should have their own storage somewhere. Keep them neat and organized—use boxes and label the supplies so anyone can find what they need for the job they are assigned to do.

I found a set of small drawers excellent for these supplies. I did not want them confused with the other library supplies, and each drawer was labeled easily. The staff appreciates this; they know where everything is at a glance. Figure 18.2 lists these items.

Figure 18.2
BOOK PROCESSING SUPPLIES

3 × 5 cards
book pockets
spine labels (or computer labels with lasting stick-to-itiveness)
date slips
good quality pen
library stamp

When you start to set up the library:

- It would be handy to have a wheelbarrow or large cart to haul boxes or stacks of books to the shelves.
- Make sure you have good light even when you are just setting up, to avoid eye strain in trying to read names and titles.
- A tape- or compact disc–player would be an addition to set-up work days— as long as nice, soothing music is played in the background!

Library Suppliers

All library suppliers have catalogues and will let you charge to a library account.

- DEMCO
  Mailing address:
  DEMCO
  P.O. Box 7488
  Madison, Wisconsin 53707-7488
  telephone 800-356-1200 (local 608-241-1201)
  Fax 800-245-1329 (local 608-241-1799)
  Internet address: http://www.demco.com
  E-mail: custserv@demco.com
- Gaylord
  Mailing Address:
  Gaylord Brothers
  Box 4901
  Syracuse, New York 13221- 4901
  Telephone 800-634-6307; Orders Telephone 800-448-6160
  Fax: 800-272-3412
- Brodart
  Mailing Address:
  Brodart Library Supplies and Furnishings
  Brodart Company
  1609 Memorial Ave.
  Williamsport, Pennsylvania 17705
  Telephone: 800-233-8959
  Internet address: http://www.brodart.com

Visit your local office supplier. Also investigate large discount stores such as Office Max, Office Depot and Wal-Mart, if nearby. See if you can establish an account with local suppliers and nearby stores. They may give the library discounts with proof of the library's nonprofit status.

19

The Library Staff

Selecting and Nurturing a Good Library Staff

Once you have decided when the library will have open hours, you will need reliable people to cover those hours. When there is no money for a salaried person, volunteers who work the desk need to be placed as carefully as if they were being paid.

Do you need a director right away? I would say no. Someone, though, should be designated head of staff, much as the core group had a chairman. This person's application should show some library experience, as well as experience in working with and leading others. The head of staff keeps a schedule of workers so all library hours are covered. The head of staff should keep track of supplies, statistics records, and the general appearance of the library.

If someone with library credentials comes forward who is willing to work as director on a volunteer basis—you are very lucky! He or she will be familiar with all of the topics covered in this handbook. There still needs to be an application on file for this person, and the library board should read it carefully. A director, even a volunteer director, represents the library in many different situations, and the board will want the finest representative they can find!

As I move on to discuss the rest of the volunteer staff I will be addressing "you," the reader, as if you are the head of an all-volunteer staff.

For other necessary staff, members of the library board may want to apply, and this is acceptable. Perhaps, though, other people from the community will be interested in volunteering to work the desk. (*See Interest/Experience of Supporters' Group, Worksheet 1.1, Appendix B.*) If necessary, post notices of when you will need people; then give interested parties the application to fill out. (Should the time come when salaries are paid, board members cannot be both board members and paid staff workers; they have to make a choice between the two.)

REQUIREMENTS AND ABILITIES

Everyone working at the library desk should be good with people of all backgrounds. The whole staff should want to welcome all patrons into the community library. They should not be judgmental about appearances or selection preferences, and they should be trustworthy since book-fine money or petty cash may be involved.

Staff members should be able to follow established daily routines and also handle situations which may arise with good humor and confidence. They must keep confidential all library records and individual borrowing habits.

If this sounds like an ideal staff member, it may be so. Why not reach for that ideal, even among volunteers? I believe that all-volunteer library staff members (no matter the jobs they undertake) need to be treated as though they were paid.

- They should fill out an application before starting work,
- There should be a conversation (interview) between the person responsible for scheduling and all applicants before they go to work.
- They need to be praised for good work and directed (diplomatically) toward doing better work when necessary.
- They must be reminded of policies and procedures when the need arises.
- They should meet together regularly to share concerns, questions and suggestions.

A sample application follows in Figure 18.1.

Figure 18.1
Example Volunteer Application Form

HANDLEBERG LIBRARY
VOLUNTEER APPLICATION FORM

Name: Last _____, First _____

Preferred Name _____   Telephone _____

Street (Physical) Address _____

Mailing Address (if different) _____

City & Zip _____

Education (Highest Level) _____

Work experience _____

Are you a "year round" resident? _____

If not, when are you here in the Handleberg area? _____

Availability for library: day(s), time of day(s) _____

_____

Have you volunteered before? If yes, where:

1. Name _____

Address _____

Telephone _____

SKILLS AND INTERESTS

Circle any area of skill or personal hobby that you might be willing to share as a Library Volunteer:

Arts/Graphics/Crafts	Homebound Services/Health
Business/Finance	Homeschooling
Office Work/Clerical	Law/Law Enforcement
Education	Library/Research
Entertainment	Technology
Environment	Skilled Trade/Construction
Gardening	Writing/Journalism

Others: (anything not listed!):

_____

Of those areas circled, please describe the level of your experience: _____

_____

Why are you interested in volunteering at the Library? _____

_____

Because every volunteer of the Handleberg Library represents the Library to the public, the Library Board and, in some instances, the whole town of Handleberg, each volunteer will present himself or herself in a professional manner, both in appearance and in performance.

Are you in agreement with the above statement? Yes _____. No _____.

Signature:_____   Date: _____

Notice how much is learned about a person from this application. Adding an interview, you would be in a good position to decide if the person might be most useful at the desk, in workroom projects, building and construction projects, on a particular committee, in an advisory position to the board, or as a story time leader.

It takes more than just the application or interview—it takes the two together. Set up a time for the interview. Does the person come on time? Is he or she dressed in an appropriate manner? Has the person filled out the application completely? Does what the applicant says he or she can do match what is on the application? What was that other volunteer experience like, and how did he or she like it? Why? Can the applicant tell you a bit about the interests and skills circled? Is the applicant willing to sign the statement at the end of the application? If not, this could tell you a whole lot about this person. He or she may not understand the importance of a library's image.

Does the applicant show an interest in this particular library—asking questions and finding out how he or she can fit in? Can this person commit to the library without listing a long line of things that may interfere?

One of my favorite stories is of the young woman who literally blew in the library door one windy March morning, full of bright gab and brilliant assurances that she would be great at doing story times and really willing to volunteer for evenings once a week. We exchanged telephone numbers, I gave her an application, she met the other staffers present, and left. The others were delighted to think they would be getting such an enthusiastic coworker. We never saw her again. Of course she had not mentioned she had to get her car fixed and she had to get her kids squared away and she had not quite finished moving her stuff here from another town, and so forth. She never returned the application, and phone calls were not returned either. We had no written information about her whatsoever. Note, though: I had not put her on the work roster or otherwise "plugged her in."

This had been sort of an application or interview in reverse: I had no application to read about her (What other volunteer experience had she? Was she here full-time? When could she start work?), but I had heard a lot about all the things she could do so well. I did not hear interested questions from her about the library, what we hoped to do, what we needed, how she could help, nothing. It was as though she had to just share all her good qualities with us, and then, feeling better, she blithely forgot the library. Moral of this story: Lots of folks can spin a good yarn (especially about themselves) but that does not guarantee a good staff worker.

Another woman called me at home to say she could volunteer four hours a week. She had been a teacher, she had volunteered for years in another library, she could do data entries on the computer, and she was delighted to know a library was growing right in her own town! Sounded like a volunteer to grab, right? I asked her to stop by and pick up an application and we set up an Interview time. Fine! She said.

She arrived a half-hour late for the interview, telling me she just knew it was not that important anyway and she had stopped to chat with a neighbor on the way over. She hadn't "bothered with" the application form because we would "get it all out now." She gabbed at me through most of the interview time, and I was hard-pressed to elicit real answers to my questions.

After finally receiving the application, I ended up asking her for four hours' training the next two Tuesdays while I was on the scene. After the second week she would "solo" with another worker.

The third week she called to say she had to visit her mother that Tuesday—was it all right? (How do you say no to that?) The fourth week (Monday night) she called to say she had a chance to play bridge on Tuesdays, so she wouldn't be able to come. We lined up another volunteer for Tuesdays and put her on short-term projects. Moral of this volunteer story: Even when they sound like a gift from heaven, they might not be so to the library.

Commitment to the library does not just mean showing up on time, every time. It also means the library comes before any personal agenda. I had a disappointing experience because I misinterpreted a fellow's reason for working at the library. He was doing data entry for me, following a local magazine through back issues, entering relevant articles so they would be useable. He spent hours hunched over the computer, professing this to be a great idea and an interesting project.

I took a look at the database one morning and found things were being entered in a much more complicated way than I had asked. There were no basic terms used. He was entering every article in every issue instead of following the categories I had set out. He was doing it his way. I suggested he modify the database so it would be simpler to search.

He never came back. He made no explanation, nor did he return telephone calls asking after his health and well-being.

I add here that he had an amazing résumé—filled with things he had done in a variety of settings across the country. I never could get him to fill out a library application form—he assured me it was all on the résumé. What I realized was that his quitting the library fit into the pattern of leaving so many other places once he found he had to conform to some sort of company plan.

On the other side of the volunteer coin, I have had staff cancel family birthday parties because of meetings, leave house guests to cover in a library emergency, come home from vacation early to make their scheduled library time, come to every staff meeting and every board meeting, and do extra work on all fundraising events. I have demanded things of them and they have responded 100 percent. They have learned about cataloguing, book processing, nonfiction, filing, shelving and confidentiality, and loved every minute of it! I love to hear them say how much they have learned. I have written recommendations for volunteers who have moved with their families to other towns with libraries.

Perhaps the volunteer success story I am fondest of concerns a lovely woman who was at first very hesitant to come and work. She was, she was sure, "too stupid" to do much good. Slowly she began to do more and more, and one day drew me aside with this statement: "I wish my mother could see me here. She always told me I was too slow to do well in school and that I would just get by. I never thought I could learn so much as I have here with you."

Commitment and responsibility are key: I think one develops a "sixth sense" about people, in the truest definition of that term. You begin to read through the glitz or chat or shyness to the core of the person. You begin to develop questions that get you the information you want. Could you tell me about your library volunteer experience? How long were you there? What kind of computer work have you done exactly? How hard might it be to work here once a week? What about your family? What do you understand about shelving books?"

WORK TIMES

Schedule two people who work well together for the same time slot at the desk. This is a good idea, in case one has to temporarily leave for some reason (restroom, emergency). Also, they can pool their knowledge and understanding of the library job. So many times, some of my staff members have said how much they learn from one another.

STAFF MEETINGS

Once a month it is a good idea to gather all the staff together—when the Library is closed, if possible—and go over concerns. Sometimes I will have a workshop or talk on some aspect of the library that will give them more insight into librarianship. Meetings usually last two to two and a half hours, although we have brought our lunches and stayed until mid-afternoon.

Everyone likes to come to these meetings because I have a printed agenda with plenty of space for them to add their own notes. They each have a notebook and so have a good record of what they have learned. I always leave plenty of time for "Others" on the agenda; the staff comes up with wonderful questions and they feel free to ask anything. If there has been a problem with a patron, or scheduling, they know they can bring it up at this time. Here is a sample agenda (I've removed work spaces) in Figure 18.2 at the top of page 139.

Staff Attitude

I have touched on this a bit already in regard to commitment, but now I want to spend just a few lines talking about staff attitude and how it affects the patrons of a library.

Figure 18.2
EXAMPLE OF A STAFF MEETING AGENDA

Staff meeting, September 29, 1999

I. Opening desk
   Take out cards due today, they will be handy when books are returned.
   Leave statistics book open nearby for easy use.

II. Checking books in
   Stack alphabetically by author's last name, Juvenile and Adult alike; do this
   other than where people are checking out books.
   Do we need to reorganize the desk top?

III. Book sale

IV. Southwest (to left, behind Biographies [you would use your local interest
   area])
   • Southwest Collection. Any marked REF may not circulate; please advise
     patrons that all others are precious and urge them to return on time.
        Includes NM, AZ, TX, border history and personalities, Chicano history,
        Apache, Navajo, Pueblo Native Americans, Southwest flora and fauna,
        special literature, art and artists, travel guides and general description,
        maps, oversize books.

V. Overdue books. *Any book not returned by the end of a day's shift is overdue.*
   File those remaining cards into the overdue stack.
   File by borrower's number, not date or author.
   This facilitates:
        • When writing people about overdues, we can find the exact number out.
        • If someone comes in wanting to know what they still have out, we can
          easily find titles by finding their card number
        • Knowing if people already have books out & overdue when they want
          more!

VI. Closing up for the day
        • Enter categories on statistics sheet *in pencil.*
        • Did you enter board books taken out? (Juvenile fiction)
        • *Alphabetize all cards by author's last name.*
        • Place in date due slot.
   Exception: *On Wed. leave cards out for evening shift. They will compile.*

VII. Junior section
        • Change books on display from time to time!
        • No more Juvenile catalogue cards: just book cards and pockets.

(continued on page 140)

(continued from page 139)

VIII. If you come in and borrow when library is not open, stamp books with next operating day's date and leave with note in statistics book for person opening next.

IX. *Notes left on desk!* Too sloppy?

Can they be placed in person's envelope instead?

Can they be placed in stats book, clipped instead of taped?

X. Questions Linda has:

1. Cards in top right-hand drawer seem to be semiduplicates of other author cards?

2. Double Biography cards, too. These need to be matched against what is actually there.

3. Yard sale things in back room.

4. Do we need to reorganize desk top for more efficiency and neatness?

Drawers are confusing?

Move supplies that aren't used everyday by everyone to back room cupboards?

5. Book sale word-of-mouth promotion, please!!

XI. Other

- The staff person who never gets up out of his or her chair to show a patron where a section or a volume is sends a message as loud as any posted notice: "I'm too busy or tired to move—find it yourself."

- The staff person who reads behind the desk or who is otherwise occupied and does not even acknowledge a patron's entrance might as well be working in the backroom out of sight.

- The staff person who acts as though everyone should know where everything is in the library signals: "What's the matter with you—you should know these things!"

- The staff person who cheerfully greets everyone who walks through the door, rises to help locate materials, inquires as to a regular patron's health, helps youngsters find a good storybook, asks questions of a student to ascertain exactly what is wanted sends the message: "I am here to help you—I am glad to do so."

Here's a loaded question: Which kind of staff member would you, as a patron, like to find when you enter a library? I maintain that even if people don't find exactly what they're looking for at a library, but receive personal attention and effort on the part of a staff member, they will be back. They have formed an impression of the library that is positive.

Impress on all staff members who interact with the pubic that staff attitude can make that big a difference. Be aware of any comments from the public that uses the library—any complaints about bad staff attitude or lack of attention to patrons should be corrected immediately.

20

Selecting Good Library
Materials from Donations

Selecting from Donations

You will undoubtedly be receiving good (and bad) donations of books and other materials before you begin purchasing new materials for the library.

CRITERIA FOR SELECTION

If you are like most libraries starting from scratch, choosing from donated materials becomes a major task. I developed a phrase for this job—selecting from donations. It became my favorite phrase as I sorted through boxes and bags and more boxes of donated books given to me (in many cases) with trembling hands and knowing smiles: there were treasures in here! I have learned to be appreciative, gracious, but firm, all at the same time. So can you!

Here are some things to consider when "selecting from" donated books:

- Are the books in clean and attractive condition?
- Are the books accurate and timely?
- Do the books fit the collection?
- Will the books provide balanced selection within a subject area?
- Do space limitations place restrictions on your choices?
- Do you have duplicates of these books?
- Do the materials form the basis of a potential historical collection?

Condition

Many times books are stored in less than ideal circumstances—cellars that flood, attics that have birds or squirrels, sheds that have bugs, or boxes where cats like to sleep with the books. Do not keep these. I have taken boxfuls to the dumpster because they were too dirty—even dangerously so—to be picked up, much less catalogued and shelved.

- Books for your library should be clean and attractive to patrons. Patrons ought not to feel they need to wash their hands after handling the books.
- Books should have their covers and should not be held together with tape or staples.
- Children's books that have been chewed, dropped in puddles or used as coloring books should not be kept.
- Books which have been underlined profusely or otherwise defaced are not what you want either.

Accuracy and Timeliness

Many people feel "if it's in the library, it must be true." This can be a downright dangerous and inaccurate notion in the case of some subjects such as health, science (space travel, rocketry, chemistry, biology), diet and nutrition, law (local and state), food preparation, and other subjects which are constantly being reexamined.

It is a good idea not to keep books on these subjects if they are more than three to five years old. For those subjects, anything older will be out of date; new information and developments have been discovered. Would you want a patron to follow a 1966 book on how to care for your heart? How about menopause? (On one library's shelf I saw one written in 1950!) It does not take a lot of explanation to see that if someone takes out a book of 1950 vintage on canning and preserving, and follows its advice, something unfortunate might occur; processes have been updated and improved since then.

Material which is not necessarily dangerous or life-affecting does not have to be kept either. It may simply be that it's out-dated and not interesting to people anymore; it is simply taking up valuable shelf room. Typical categories are sewing and fashion books; some arts and crafts idea books; outdoor camping and the accompanying equipment suggestions; interior decoration; get-rich-quick schemes (sometimes these can be dangerous, too!); and fads in religion, psychology, the occult, business management, résumé writing, secretarial skills and parenting.

Fitting into the Collection

When you decide what your library's role in the community is to be (see Chapter 4), you are, in one sense, already on the way to starting a selection policy.

If you are primarily recreational in role, then your emphasis will not be on deep reference and nonfiction. You should be guided basically by what people in your community may need and want: the Community Assessment (see Chapter 7) and Interests/Expectation of Supporters' Group list (*see Worksheet 1.1, Appendix B*) will both help you decide what subjects to have on the nonfiction shelves.

Of course, once the library gets rolling, you will get a better idea of needs and wants; for now we're just dealing with the donations in the fastest and fairest way we can.

A thought: Sometimes we come upon a book that is interesting but bears no relationship to needs, but it "calls to us." It may be an unusual art book, a travel book on some faraway exotic location, a humorous treatise on something, or—in the case of children's books—a story with a setting or art work far removed from a local child's experience. I call such books "expanders," and tend to listen to my instinct. They broaden the library's collection, and may open up a whole new world to people who read. Go with your instincts when they speak to you—just do not go overboard; be able to explain why these particular books get to stay.

Balanced Selection

Try to include information on several aspects in a given area. In religion, for example, even if you are given 50 volumes on the Catholic Church, try to limit the number you keep to be in line with the number you may have on the Protestant or other faiths. Another example: You do not need to keep all 30 cookbooks limited to low-calorie cooking. Keep enough to balance the cookbook section. Again, you do not need to keep 15 books on speaking Russian (or any language) if you only have one or two volumes on other languages, and especially if Russian is not spoken in your particular geographic area.

Space Limitations

Library shelving is always at a premium. Do not be talked into thinking shelves must be filled immediately. It may seem to you or to well-meaning donors that you will never fill the shelves, but believe me, you will.

You want good books, not just any books. As long as there are spaces on the shelves, there will be room for useful and appropriate books. This is of course especially true of the nonfiction.

Adult fiction can be treated a little differently. Because many larger libraries have to weed their fiction to make room for new titles, older titles and old authors disappear never to return. It is a treat to go into a library where these titles and authors still live and are available.

A group who was dealing with hundreds of donations had the natural wisdom to put every novel on the shelf. Accordingly, their collection goes from the 1930s to the present day, and many patrons comment—with joy—on finding authors' works they have not been able to get in years. This is one of the benefits of having donations to select from; you receive books you can no longer buy from vendors.

With children's books, you can never have too many of one title, one subject or one illustrator. Children are voracious readers and will read the same books over and over. Sometimes friends will want the same title—having more than one on the shelf is just what they hope for! Cleanliness is the major consideration for children's books. I also don't like to keep books advertising products. If the toy or product came first, before the books were printed as promotions, I define the book as an advertisement. Examples are McDonald's, Barbie, M & M's, Ninja Turtles, and so forth. Take a look at the story: If the product is primary and the story secondary, put it in the book sale.

Duplicates

You do not need many duplicate copies of the same titles in a small library. Exceptions would be titles in the children's section or very popular current authors' works. Some authors are popular in more than one reader group. Copies of their works can be placed in several places: Stephen King and V. C. Andrews are examples of this. Duplicates of basic reference books (dictionaries, almanacs) or some local history titles (you can circulate one and not the other) are not unusual.

Most people leaving donations understand, though, when you say, "We already have this title, but I'm sure it will sell well at the book sale."

Potential Historical Collection

Sometimes books covering earlier periods of our human history can provide invaluable glimpses into those times. If this idea appeals to you and your library group, decide for yourselves at what year or event you will stop saving old books: World War I? The Roaring Twenties? The Depression?

I have chosen the end of World War II as my limit. My decision was made for me when we were given some fine first-person accounts of battles in Europe. These books are no longer published and the general accounts available today cannot touch these older ones for pathos.

I also keep books which show what life was like in the late 1800s, the 1920s, the Depression, and stateside during both World Wars. There are health books, law books, school books (illustrated), home economy guides, agricultural how-to's, cookbooks, an encyclopedia (1889), and some others with just plain wonderful covers typical of their era. I do not keep every book in this time period; I have created guidelines here, too, and so should you.

Hopefully, this fascinating collection will someday be housed (noncirculating) in an historical section of the library and will prove interesting and helpful to those wanting to see how things have changed from those earlier days. You could do the same thing; someone in the community would probably enjoy taking charge of such a collection.

Just because books are old doesn't mean they have value of any kind, although there are lots of people waiting to tell you they do. To those people who tell me that all old books have value and should be kept, I say, "Come to the book sale and start your own historical collection!"

Here's an example of how to put all this into your selection policy:

> All donated books will be considered for their usefulness and appropriateness to the whole collection. Handleberg Library will make every effort to incorporate useful donated books into its collection. There are, however, times when this is not possible.

Things to Be Prepared for as You Select

"WHERE'S MY BOOK?"

There will be those who are sure their books will be selected and will come checking to see if you have put "their books" on your shelves. Let me share two good illustrations of this:

A very distinguished gentleman gave a library a set of leather-bound classics with pride in his eyes and a very positive tone of voice. "I know you'll want these," he said, refusing the proffered donation form which said donations could be sold if not used unless the donor wanted them back. These books, although attractive, were not practical for circulation. They brought a nice price from a book dealer, and new, circulating books were purchased.

About a year later, the gentleman brought his granddaughter in to see the books he had given. Of course he was angered not to find them and demanded to know where they were. When told, he said he would never darken the library's door again. If only he had read the donation receipt form!

I remember being looked in the eye by a diminutive white-haired lady who stated—after looking over the gardening section—that she " didn't see that book about onions that we gave the library over there." I had been working in this particular library for about two years and was beginning to recognize the direction in which she was headed.

"When would that have been?" I asked.

"Well, that was before my husband died in 1967," she responded. "We gave that book because he grew onions and it told what you could do with them."

Fortunately, for me, it had not been my doing (it was now 1988) that the onion book had obviously been weeded. I tried to tell her it might well have been replaced by a more modern one on uses of onions, but my explanation met with frosty looks and shakes of the head. To her mind—and to many others—no book needs to be taken from the library shelf, no matter how old or outdated.

These stories underline why I suggest you make it plain when people give books that you will be selecting from the donations, and that you create a donation policy, and a donation form. (See Chapter 15.)

One rather maligned part of building and maintaining a good collection for any library, no matter the size, is the job of weeding. This job is detested by some and embraced by others. Regardless of its popularity, however, it must be done to keep the collection current with the times, relevant to the community, and to keep shelf space available for new titles.

"WEEDING? OH, YOU SHOULDN'T DO THAT!"

Just as you now are plowing through boxes of donations and weeding out ones to keep, in a year or so space limitations may demand that you weed the shelves. This is selecting with a reverse twist. You will be looking for volumes to take *off* the shelf. That is weeding. You will be using the same criteria that we used in selecting from donations in the first part of this chapter.

People may shudder when you say you are doing it, but do not be cowed. You are weeding out books no longer accurate, clean, or useful, and getting rid of them so better ones can take their place!

"WHAT'LL WE DO WITH THE BOOKS WE DON'T WANT?"

Book stores have sale tables to get rid of books that are not selling well. A library can get rid of books that aren't useful to the collection:

- Have a book sale corner or bookcase in the library as a steady source of income.
- Have a book sale once or twice a year, depending on storage space and how many strong arms and backs you can call on.
- Have a paperback swap shelf where people bring one in, take one out— or how ever many they want.
- See if there is an institution who could use your discarded books—pris-

ons, juvenile homes, halfway houses.

- Let people who are deep into recycling take the books to recycling centers.
- Give them to whoever can use them.

When you accept donations, you will need a ready answer for those who assure you the library will be better off keeping these books. I hope this chapter has afforded you some good responses. Feel free to copy me by using my "We select from all donations" phrase. And then whip out the donation receipt form and have them sign it!

21

Buying New
Library Materials

As you get ready to order from the sources I suggest in this chapter, here are some things you may be asked to do and some things I suggest you do.

- You may need to provide proof of your nonprofit status.

  You can establish nonprofit status by contacting your state and federal tax bureaus. Not all vendors ask for proof of this, but you want to be ready when one does. This can be a lengthy process, so start early.

- You will need to set up an account and get an account number in advance of the first order.

- You may be asked to write a letter to the company using the library's letterhead. A sample ends this chapter in Figure 21.1.

- You may need to have a credit card for charging books.

- You may need to create an official purchase order form with the library's name on it.

- I suggest you make a folder for each book business you use. Keep accurate records of purchase orders, packing slips, receipts, and cancelled checks.

Where Can You Get Books?

There is a whole variety of book seller options awaiting you as you begin to buy new books for the collection. These can be jobbers, book publishers, large bookstore chains, Internet vendors, local bookstores and discount stores.

JOBBERS

- Jobbers are vendors who buy in great volume from the publishing houses. They sell primarily to libraries and schools, and provide varying discounts on all titles, dependent on what they paid themselves.
- All publishers' titles may not be available through one jobber; you may need to contact another jobber or the publisher directly.
- Jobbers offer processing for libraries (print all cards, pockets, spine labels, apply book jacket protective covers, prepare bar-coding and provide computer records for the catalogue system.
- They have available a variety of formats: books, video cassettes, audio book cassettes, large print books, and bilingual material.
- They do not charge tax to libraries; they may or may not ship free of charge.
- They can be reached by mail, telephone, fax or through the Internet. Telephone orders will enable you to know if titles are immediately available.
- The two most prominent jobbers are:
    1. Ingram Library Services, Inc.
       Telephone: 800-937-5116
       Internet address: http://www.ingramlibrary.com
    2. Baker & Taylor Information and Entertainment Services
       Telephone: 800-775-1800
       Internet address: http://www.baker-taylor.com
- You will need to set up an account with the jobbers and receive an account number before placing the first order.
- Service can be very fast.
- They will send the bill after the shipment is made.
- Jobbers will happily provide all sorts of catalogues and descriptions of their services.

Read what they send you. Ask questions and make sure you understand everything before ordering. Make sure you understand how much discount you will receive on your orders. Decide if you want "back ordering" or not. Back ordering means if they are out of a title when you order it, they will ship the title later when they get it in. Sometimes this can be months.

Keep a file for each vendor, including all orders you place, packing slips, receipts and cancelled checks.

Always get the name of the person with whom you set up your account or placed your order; jot down the day and time you called.

BOOK PUBLISHERS

- You can order titles directly from the publisher.
- Some publishers offer library discounts; you will need to ask each one.
- Publishers should be able to provide you with catalogues of their titles in print as well as upcoming titles.
- Names, addresses and telephone numbers are available on the Internet and in the *Writer's Digest*.

Ordering directly from a publisher works well on specialty books such as professional titles, unusual or local nonfiction and sets of books. Indeed, sometimes the publisher is the only source for these. Always state you are a nonprofit library, ask for library rate, and for their current catalogue.

Keep a file for each vendor, including all orders you place, packing slips, receipts and cancelled checks.

Always get the name of the person with whom you set up your account or placed your order; jot down the day and time you called.

LARGE BOOKSTORE CHAINS

These are the "big guys" of bookstores, the places that also offer cappuccino and pastries while you fill your book list. Some examples are: Barnes & Noble, Borders Books & Music, and large bookstore chains local to your particular state or area.

- These usually give a 20 percent library discount on paperbacks and hardbacks.
- These stores sometimes have wonderful sale tables with books for all ages. Prices can range from $0.99 to $6.95 and your dollars can go far.
- You can buy from them in person or on-line.
- They will require proof of nonprofit status (federal form).
- An application must be on file with them prior to first purchase.
- The library must have a purchase order form for the bill to be sent to the library, otherwise there must be payment at time of sale.

Some franchises of these bookstore chains are better than others, depending on their individual store's manager. Do not assume they are all alike. Do not assume that they have all the titles on any and all subjects, either; *they carry what sells best for them.*

It is always safest to go with a list of specific needs, subject- or author-wise, to avoid picking up things that may look good but are not what you are really after. These are some of the best places to get the hot new best-sellers if your readers are panting for them. The discount can be as high as 30 percent on the *New York Times Bestseller List.* If the store is within a short trip, it is a good deal. (The fastest place is an Internet vendor). I do not advise ordering from these stores unless all other avenues have been tried; special orders are not discounted.

Make sure you tell the register clerk you will be using your library account *before* she checks you out.

Keep a file for each vendor, including all orders, bills, receipts, packing slips and cancelled checks.

One thing I love to do in these big stores is browse through the juvenile section. You can see and hold a book to decide if it is really as good as the review or worth the price.

I often work from a list of books that I think I want to buy—look at them in the store, and then order them through the jobber. This is especially handy with all the new series books that are coming out: some are just fluff, but some are good.

INTERNET VENDORS

Several on-line booksellers are in operation, and the Internet bookstore most customers agree has the best reputation at this time is Amazon. Its Internet address is http://www.Amazon.com. A good site for both new and used books, as well as some out of print titles, is Powells at www.powells.com.

Barnes & Noble retail also has an on-line store with a site at http://www.barnesandnoble.com. The same can be said for Borders Books & Music, located at http://www.borders.com.

- The Internet discounts vary and are competitive, but they do not offer extra discounts to libraries.
- You establish an account over the Internet.
- Titles are searched, chosen, and orders placed on-line; you know immediately if they have the title.
- Shipping is charged.
- Orders can be tracked.
- Service is very fast. (Priority Mail)

Keep a file for each vendor, including all orders, bills, receipts, packing slips and cancelled checks.

LOCAL BOOKSTORES

Some towns, even small ones, have a local bookseller who would like to help the library out.

- They may be able to offer 20 percent discount on best-sellers. Other discounts will depend on the individual case.
- You will need to set up an account with them, and they may want a letter with the library letterhead on it for their file. This may serve as a purchase order form.
- I do not advise ordering through the local bookstore, unless they will give you a discount (other places are cheaper) or it is a special local title.
- They may be interested in hosting an author book-signing in the library, with the author donating a copy to the library.
- Keep a file for the store, including all orders, bills, receipts, packing slips and cancelled checks.

DISCOUNT STORES

By discount stores I mean those who may have a book section or have book sale bins. The discount store whose name first springs to mind is Wal-Mart, but there may be others in your area (Target, K-Mart, etc.). Approach the manager with a letter (library letterhead on it) and ask what they can do for nonprofit organizations like yours. You will need to show proof of the library's nonprofit status.

Keep a file for each store, including all orders, bills, receipts, packing slips and cancelled checks.

Figure 21.1 provides a sample "official" letter:

Figure 21.1
SAMPLE BUSINESS LETTER

HANDLEBERG LIBRARY
200 Main Street
Handleberg, Your State 90003

Mr. Harold Berg, Mgr.
Your Store
100 W. Park
Handleberg, YS

Dear Mr. Berg:

The Handleberg Library is interested in purchasing books and other library-related items from your store. We would like a chance to meet with you to discuss this possibility.

Handleberg Library has filed for and received nonprofit status with both the state and the IRS. We attach a Form _____ which lists out number as _____.

We will call to set up an appointment, and look forward to meeting with you.

Until then, I am

Sincerely,

Mrs. Margaret Hines
President, Handleberg Library Board of Trustees

Handleberg Library Hours: M–F 10–6
Tel: 000-0000

I hope this has given you enough information to feel ready and eager to begin purchasing new books. I stress recordkeeping as essential because you may be spending money from several sources; it is good business to be able to show where it went. It is also prudent to have proof of order and payment handy in case of a mix-up in orders or a problem with billing and payment.

— PART FIVE —
LIBRARY NUTS AND BOLTS

22

Daily Procedures in the Library

This chapter will cover:

- Opening and closing—create a good routine
- Circulation statistics—why we need them and how to do them
- Registering new patrons
- Checking materials in and out
- Confidentiality—privacy of records and minding our own business.

When I first arrived on the scene at one library, the volunteers had been struggling to do the right things. They claimed they did not really know what they were doing—they were just doing it. I asked for questions and almost everyone in the group had good, helpful questions all having to do with the nuts and bolts of library routine. With the exception of confidentiality, their concerns are reflected in the above list.

My suggestions all attempt to simplify and certainly demystify what running a library is all about, at least on the day-to-day level. All procedures can be quickly learned and will help to put people at ease in their daily volunteer jobs as library staff.

159

Opening and Closing

Create a good routine for opening and closing the Library. It will help eliminate racing around at the beginning and end of a busy day "trying to remember what I'm supposed to do!" People can relax when instructions are written down.

Write your routine in terms as clear as possible and post it where all staff can refer to the instructions. It should be used as a checklist each day until everyone has it memorized. Figure 22.1 shows a sample (you will want to make yours fit your own building):

Figure 22.1
SAMPLE PROCEDURE LIST

HANDLEBERG LIBRARY
PROCEDURES FOR OPENING LIBRARY,
CHECKING IN BOOKS AND END OF DAY

OPENING
 1. Hang sign outside and turn OPEN sign on door.
 2. Turn up heat.
 3. Turn on lights.
 4. Unlock back door (same key for both doors).
 5. Bring in books from drop box.
 6. Change date on stamp to two weeks from today's date.
 7. If holiday, advance one more day.
 8. Take out book cards for items due today.
 9. Open statistics book to remind yourself what needs counting.
10. Check staff notices on wall near window.
11. Check your personal envelope, if you have one, for notes and messages.
12. Books in Book Drop and on Return cart at front of desk:

   • Find corresponding book card under due date.

   • Put book card in book, removing date card (put back in box on desk).

   • After all books are recarded, separate for Juvenile, Adult Fiction, Nonfiction, Biography.

   • Reshelve: Nonfiction by number (if there is one written on card or spine) and Fiction by author's last name.

IF UNSURE, LEAVE IN A PILE SO MARKED FOR NEXT STAFF PERSON. IT IS BETTER NOT TO SHELVE THAN TO SHELVE INCORRECTLY!

END OF DAY

Count how many books in each category went out. Enter number in statistics book.

Alphabetize all book cards together by author's last name.

Put book cards behind due date showing on cards.

Fill out rest of statistics sheet.

Then, work backwards from number 4 (above) to number 1.

GOOD LUCK AND THANK YOU!

This kind of map through the day has been a big success for the staff I work with; they used it daily until they did not need it anymore. Since everyone does things the same way, cards are not misplaced, books were shelved better (so they can be found!) and statistics were entered with understanding and care.

Circulation Statistics

What are the daily statistics all libraries need to keep?

- How many people walk through the library door for any reason each day?
- How many items go out (circulate) each Open day in these categories:
    Adult fiction
    Juvenile fiction
    Nonfiction (split adult and juvenile, or both together)
    Magazines
    Videos
    Audio books

- How many reference questions do you answer each day
    About library related things
    About your community?
        Example: Where is the road to Harpswell, how old is this town, can you tell me where I can buy lunch?

- How many hours open that day?
- Who worked?

Figure 22.2 provides a sample statistics sheet (enter rows for all open days):

Figure 22.2
EXAMPLE OF A STATISTICS SHEET

HANDLEBERG LIBRARY
DAILY STATISTIC SHEET FOR MONTH OF August, 1999.

Date	Patron visits	Adult FIC	A. NF	J. books	Internet users	Ref. L./C.	Hours Open	Workers
1	43	20	14	15	5	20	6	MS, FG
2	25	14	5	13	6	10	6	PP, RJ
TOTAL								

Of course this will be done by hand unless you have it on a computer. Count everything in each category—if you give a story time, count the books read and each person (adult and child) who attends. If you have an evening program for adults at the library, count each person in attendance in the patron column. If the same patron comes in twice, count each time. You count an Internet user twice, as both patron and Internet user.

As you can see, neatness counts. The one adding up the column at month's end will appreciate it! At the end of the month, the "TOTAL" row gives the month's record. At fiscal year's end, those rows can be added for a grand total.

"Why Do We Need to Do This?"

• You will doubtless be required to keep and give statistics such the ones above if you want to receive any available funding from your state library. Many state libraries—if not all—require some sort of annual report from their libraries. This assumes—and I will go into this later—that you will want to connect to your state's library.

• Many other funding sources you might want to investigate will need to see your track record, so to speak. If you provide comparison figures, it should show your growth (in patron number, in circulation). Increasing figures in Internet use, for example, will help prove your request for more technology money. Increased use of nonfiction may help raise money for that part of the collection.

- Your local government will be interested in seeing how you are serving people—how many people visit you on an average day, if they are paying for your collection in part or in whole and what is being used most.
- The board should be able to make a statistical report at any time about the library's service.
- One last good reason for keeping statistics, especially the Reference question column (as it pertains to library use), is that you can see where you need to improve within the library. Keeping a list of often-asked questions such as subject areas students seek, requested titles, Internet searching, and where things are kept can help you make changes within the library collection and service.

Registering New Patrons

You may have patron cards commercially printed, or you can order them through a library supplier. In case you do neither, Figure 22.3 is a sample registration procedure to follow, using blank cards.

Figure 22.3
EXAMPLE FOR PROCESSING NEW PATRON CARDS

HANDLEBERG LIBRARY
REGISTRATION OF NEW PATRONS

Get out a new white 3 × 5 card and the next Handleberg Library card which should already have its number (#). (Start first library card with number 001.)

  1. Print patron information on white card (or have patron do it):

    Last name, first name, initial
    Physical Address
    Mailing Address , if different
    Town, State, Zip
    Telephone, Today's date
    Library card number (staff will enter this)

(continued on page 164)

(continued from page 163)

2. Enter the next library card number on patron's new library card.
3. Enter today's date on the patron's new library card.
4. Give the library card to the new patron and say thank you!
   Hand the patron a bookmark with library hours listed, and ask if you can give the patron a tour.
5. Enter last name and library card number on Rolodex file card.
6. File patron card in proper place.

Checking Materials In and Out

DEFINITIONS

- Book card—card that is in book with title and other information.
- Date slip or grid—the place where the due date is stamped.
- Library card—card patron has with individual library card number on it.

PROCEDURE

- Staff puts patron library card number on book card.
- Staff stamps due date on book card and on date slip or grid.
- Give patron book, thanking the patron and repeating the due date.
- Keep book cards in a pile for statistics count. (See Opening and Closing procedure.)
- Finally, put all book cards in alphabetical order by author and put in box or tray behind date they are due.

Confidentiality

Every effort should be made to keep all library records secure and private. That is why a rolodex file should only have patron name and library card number in it—not other information about the patron. Patron registration cards should be kept out of reach for anyone not working at the desk. Overdue cards—even though they only have patron library card number on them—should be kept filed securely, with no lists posted about overdue materials or fine-owing patrons.

Having a confidentiality policy is very important and should be done long before the library doors open for business. The policy should be shown to every volunteer and hung in a prominent place in the library for all patrons to see, also.

This policy should state unequivocally that all library records are private and will not be revealed by any staff member to anyone, under any circumstances. Figure 22.4 following is an example of such a policy.

Figure 22.4
SAMPLE CONFIDENTIALITY POLICY

HANDELBERG LIBRARY
CONFIDENTIALITY POLICY

- The Handleberg Library holds in strict confidence all information on registered patrons and their borrowing records. Under no circumstances will staff or Board Members of the Library divulge information about book titles borrowed, telephone numbers of borrowers, addresses of borrowers or any other information which may be requested by a third party for whatever reason.
- The Library respects the right of privacy to which its borrowers are entitled.
- The Handleberg Library adheres to the *Library Bill of Rights*, as written by the American Library Association; a copy is posted.

Adopted by the Handleberg Library Board of Trustees, May 21, 1999.

It is a revelation to some staff members to learn that talking about which books some of their neighbors borrow from the library is wrong. It is wrong because what people borrow is their own business and no one else's.

In small towns, the old saying is: Everybody knows everybody else's business. Those of us who live in small towns can not only agree on that saying, but can probably provide strong evidence as to its truth. Libraries do not broadcast news about patrons, what fines they may owe, books they lose, and especially about what titles they borrow or what topics they research.

When I first was Director in a small library years ago, the town's population was about 500. One of the long-time staff members claimed to know every generation of every family. It was her great delight to go to social gatherings and regale folks with how much so-and-so owed on overdue books, or what somebody's daughter was reading now.

I received word of this one day shortly after starting work when a listener to these tales came in and commiserated with me on how much money was owed to the library by a patron (even named the patron!). I was surprised, and became uneasy when another patron was mentioned as owing money. When asked, he told me where he had gotten his information and assured me that "We all love hearing about the library."

Needless to say, I had a staff meeting and corrected the situation. My talkative staff member had never thought she was spreading confidential information. I explained to her that people's records with us were to be kept in confidence even if the sheriff arrived.

When we loan books (or videos, or audio books, or even when we search for Internet sites), we keep our patrons' tastes and preferences within the library walls. Not many libraries have people actually sign their names anymore on the circulation cards; numbers either written by hand or computerized, are used. In this way, the next person cannot tell who has borrowed that item before.

Rolodexes with names and library numbers on them should not be available to patrons on the other side of the desk. Notices about delinquent patrons, problem patrons or any kind of list including patron names (for whatever reason) should not be tacked up where the world can see them. (I hate those bad check lists you see in supermarkets!)

Patrons—especially young people—should feel safe in borrowing materials dealing with subjects they need to know about at a particular time in their life. Perhaps the library is the one place where they can voice a question about birth control, beauty treatments, mental health, diet, death, drugs and get information without a lecture or a laugh attached to it. And just as their requests are honored in an adult way, so the staff does not gossip to their parents or pals about what they have requested.

Parents sometimes say they have a right to know what books their children are taking out. They may ask you to check and let them know so they can make sure the children get the material back on time. When you have decided what age a child can have his or her own library card, that is the age after which you do not tell parents the titles their children check out. In the case of overdues, you can simply tell the parents how many titles are checked out—not the titles themselves. I hate to say this, but if it becomes a problem, then the parent had better accompany the child to the library to oversee the selection of books.

23

Keywords Used
in Processing Materials

At this point, I want to give you a list of words I will be using frequently from now on. They have to do with all the steps in identifying, shelving and circulating—in other words, *processing*—the collection you have been selecting and purchasing.

- Fiction—works that are *not true*. Included here are novels of all types: science fiction, historical novels, horror, fantasy, westerns, mysteries, romances.
- Nonfiction—works that are about *true things*. Included here are biographies, science, health, reference books, history, art, arts and crafts, religion, philosophy, pet care, space travel, books about the law, cooking, local history. These books usually circulate .

  Please try to get these two straight in your mind. People are easily confused by them. Mainly, I believe, because nonfiction sounds like not true. It is, however, exactly the opposite! Fiction is false (f/f), nonfiction is not false (n/f).

- Reference—nonfiction works used for fact-finding. Most typically included are almanacs, encyclopedias, dictionaries, telephone books, government rosters, record books, state information, motor vehicle regulations. These volumes do not circulate and are shelved together.

- Spine label—a permanent label affixed on the spine of books, audio books and videos where classification information is placed. This information tells people where the book is placed in the library, on the shelf, and also what format it is in.
- Book pocket—pocket for holding the book card in the back of the library book. It is usually high-backed with a date grid for use with date stamp.
- Book strip—oaktag (a type of paper) strip placed inside the back cover, aligned with lower edge and right side and glued on the two edges; the book card is slipped inside.
- Date slip—a commercial product available through library supplier which has a stick-on backing and a grid for dates due.
- Book card—a plain 3 × 5 style card which identifies the book and stays in the library when book is borrowed; book card fits vertically into book pocket.
- Catalogue card—a plain 3 × 5 card used horizontally. It contains all information about the book. There are from three to five of these for every book in the library. Automated systems make these obsolete, except for shelf list card (see Chapter 25).
- Library stamp—a rubber stamp custom made by any stamp outfit with the library name, address and telephone number on it. Above that information could be "Please return this book to:" or "This book property of:" Some libraries include their hours, too.
- Date stamp—one of those adjustable rubber stamps with months, days of the month and the year. If all materials are loaned for the same time period (two to three weeks) only one stamp is needed. If you have more than one loan period (one week for popular titles or videos, two weeks for everything else) you will need more stamps so you do not have to keep changing your only one.
- Large paperback—these are any paperbound books larger than the familiar paperback books (7 × 5). They may be regular novel size or larger (12 × 10, or so).

In the next chapter, we go to the library areas, covering the quick way to shelve, identify and circulate the appropriate materials to each. If there is some repetition, it probably will not hurt to hear it again as some methods apply in all areas.

24

Processing:
Shelving, Identifying
and Circulating

Volunteer library groups can shelve, identify and circulate books and other materials by following some basic rules. My goal here is not to give a course in cataloguing and shelf order, but instead to give the quick and simple lowdown on how to make materials quickly accessible to the patrons.

I will refer to the Dewey Decimal System only in the simplest terms possible. Those who are so inclined can go on and learn the more advanced methods that librarians know. In Appendix A, I include a schedule from Dewey that will be useful to you as you pursue real cataloguing.

Let's now go to the library areas, covering the quick way to shelve, identify and circulate the appropriate materials to each.

Reference

The following are the basic reference materials commonly found in library reference sections:

- Almanacs, dictionaries, thesauruses, encyclopedia sets
- Telephone books, community lists or directories, local rosters
- State publications, motor vehicle regulations

There may be other materials from your particular locale which you may wish to classify as REF, depending on their cost, out-of-print status, high demand or need of staff assistance. Examples are local histories no longer in print, SAT study books, state and federal tax workbooks, volumes listing associations, businesses, colleges and military service requirements.

IDENTIFYING

For each volume, on a spine label, put the word in its title (or abbreviation) underneath REF as follows:

REF
TEL (telephone books)

REF
ALM (almanacs)

REF
DIC (dictionaries)
(If you have more than one kind)

REF
DIC-E , (English dictionary) or DIC- S (Spanish dictionary)

REF
GOV (government)

REF
HAN (Handleberg's local information; use your town's initials)

SHELVING

Reference volumes can be temporarily shelved in the order they are most frequently used:

- Place booklets, pamphlets and 8 × 11 lists in slim 3-hole notebooks for protection and better shelving.
- Mark the area on the shelves where each category goes so they are put back in the same place, using the abbreviations from spine labels.

This is a simple, easy to maintain system; make up your own abbreviations if you wish, but make them clear to the staff. Later on each volume will each need its own Dewey or Library of Congress number and will be shelved in that numerical order.

CIRCULATION

Traditionally, reference materials do not leave the library; they do not circulate. Instead, they are used in-house, within the library, at study tables or in the reading area. Reference materials are also traditionally expensive to replace; keeping them in the library avoids their theft or loss. In-house use insures that questions can be answered from these materials at any time. Make the noncirculating status of reference materials clear to the public and staff:

- Inside, on the pocket, place notification that the work is "NOT FOR CIRCULATION." This will remind the staff that the volume cannot leave the library.
- The book card (clearly marked REF in upper left corner) can then be left at the desk (with the patron's library card number) if you want to keep track of where that volume is during the day, or how many reference volumes are used.

Newspapers and Periodicals

IDENTIFYING

Each should be marked with the library stamp and receive a large white sticker (those used for homemade pickles and preserves are fine!) where the return date can be placed.

SHELVING

Newspapers and periodicals should be neatly stacked with the most recent edition or issue uppermost on the pile. Decide how many issues of the volume you want to keep available—one month, six months, a year.

CIRCULATION

Find a file box for 3 × 5 cards to keep at the desk. Use this for all periodicals and newspaper cards. One card in this box should have the title of one magazine, and so forth. When someone borrows the periodical, the date of the issue, patron number, and date due can all be entered for recordkeeping as in Figure 24.1.

Figure 24.1
EXAMPLE OF A PERIODICAL CARD

Handleberg Gazette

Issue Date	Patron Number	Due Date
6/11/99	235	7/1/99

Videos

These popular library materials have heavy use and lots of handling, so you want to make them easy to circulate and re-shelve.

IDENTIFYING VIDEOS

- On each video, underneath V-F (Video-Fiction), V-NF or V-J, write the first letter of the title on the spine label.
- Do not alphabetize by *A*, *An*, or *The*; instead, go to the next word in the title. Examples are:

  Dances with Wolves = D

  Alien = A

  The Secret Garden = S

  A Bridge Too Far = B

  Note that *3 Men and a Baby* would be shelved before the A's, as would all numerals in their own order (1, 2, 3).
- Buy a thick three-ring loose-leaf notebook and see-through protective sleeve pages to fit.
- Make a copy of the descriptive covers of each video and put them into the sleeves.
- Arrange these pages alphabetically by first letter of title. Do not alphabetize by *A*, *An*, or *The*; go to the next word in the title.
- Make sections in the notebook by placing tabs for fiction (FIC), nonfiction (NF) and Children's (J), if you have videos for any or all of these.
- This notebook creates a video collection catalogue for patrons to browse through, even if some titles are circulating at that moment.

SHELVING

Arrange videos for the shelf in the same order used in the notebook; mark the sections as you did in the notebook (FIC, NF, and J) to make shelving easier. Each section has its own titles arranged from numerals to Z. An example is shown in Figure 24.2 of a spine label and video card.

Figure 24.2
EXAMPLES OF VIDEO SPINE LABEL
AND VIDEO CARD

V = NF	V = NF
S	S
	Smokey the Bear
	Patron # Due date
	254 6/24/99

CIRCULATION

- Patrons bring video to desk for check out.
- In a single file box have all video cards (like book cards) alphabetically arranged first by section and title.
- Take out appropriate card, enter patron number and date due.
- Refile card in back of box after a divider tabbed: Videos OUT (no sections).
- When video is returned, refile video card alphabetically with others in proper section for next circulation.

Audio Books

IDENTIFYING

While it is not imperative to do so, if you can afford to buy plastic cases for these cassettes, the audio book's life will be extended. However, using rubberbands to keep audio book boxes closed and asking patrons to use special care at home should be sufficient to keeping them safe and circulating.

Regardless of whether you purchase cases or use the box the audio book comes in, here are identification suggestions:

- For fiction, on the spine label put AB (for audio book), and under it FIC (fiction). Beneath that put the first three initials of the author's last name.
- For nonfiction, use AB, the Dewey number and the author's initials.

SHELVING

Audio books can be either fiction or nonfiction and are shelved by the author's name or nonfiction number. They can be placed spine out on shelves, or cover out on racks. Audio books may be shelved with the books, have their own section, or share space with the videos. They can be for adults and for children. Sample audio book spine label and audio card is shown in Figure 24.3.

Figure 24.3
EXAMPLES OF AUDIO BOOK SPINE LABEL
AND AUDIO CARD

```
        AB
        FIC
        MOR
```

```
AB
FIC
MOR     Morrison, Toni
Beloved
5 cass.


Patron #        Due date
197              6/13/99
```

CIRCULATION

- On the audio book card place all the same information you put on the spine label.
- On the card write out the full author name (last name first) and title.
- Underneath note how many cassettes are in the set.
- Audio book cards are used and filed along with book cards.

• Always check the box or case before letting an audio book circulate: make sure all tapes are there. This precaution should be repeated when the audio book is returned to the library.

Children's Collection

I have a general word about this, *the most important part* of the library's collection: The children who use it today can be the adult patrons of the future. If you give the collection and its patrons good care and feeding, these young people will develop a library habit as they travel from this area to the other library areas. Try to allot a large segment of the library budget to children's books, audio books and other props which enhance the collection: puppets, posters, pictures of authors, and high quality videos.

Identifying

With the possible exception of early readers, public libraries do not usually identify books by grade level; they leave that sort of definition to the school libraries. Sometimes defining a book's reading or grade level keeps a child from trying a book of a higher grade level—a book which could delight and challenge that child. Instead, public libraries try to develop a love of reading in a variety of book categories.

So how can a public library identify a children's collection, if not by grade or reading level?

There are several "family members" or categories of books that children expect to find in their section of the library. Figure 24.4 presents some of those types with their codes and spine label.

Figure 24.4
SAMPLE CHILDREN'S BOOK CODING

TYPE OF BOOK	CODE ON BOOK CARD	SPINE LABEL
Picture Books Red = more text story; Yellow = more picture story	Color code (marker) Author initial	Red or yellow tape S

(continued on page 176)

(continued from page 175)

TYPE OF BOOK	CODE ON BOOK CARD	SPINE LABEL
Board Books (thick card-cardboard pages for baby's hands	BB	BB
Early Reader books	ER Author's name	ER HOB
Nonfiction	Number + j Author's name	568j PRO
Juvenile Biographies	J B Subject's last name	J B EDI
Series	J Author's name, no. of title in series	J KEE 89
Juvenile Novels	J FIC Author's name	J FIC WIL
Juvenile Reference	REFj	REFj DIC-E

Each category should each have its own space or section within the children's area, with the space clearly labeled.

SHELVING

- All juvenile fiction books are shelved by the author's single last name initial.
- Nonfiction and biographies are treated in the nonfiction section of this chapter.
- Using the table above, divide the collection into categories.
- Make spine labels for each book, using the spine label column in Figure 24.2.
- Shelve books in their appropriate alphabetical or numerical order within their own spaces on the shelves.

For suggestions of creative shelving, please see Chapter 12, section on Furniture.

CIRCULATION

"How-to's" are covered jointly with YA and Adult materials in last section, "Circulation."

Recommending Children's Titles

I recommend you not say to a child, "You can't read that yet" or, "That's too easy for you!" Instead, ask what sort of stories a youngster enjoys. Remember, they may be following a strict reading program in school—this may be the place they come to read for the love of it! Perhaps, too, someone reads to them, or they read to younger siblings.

It is well-documented that children love to hear or read their favorites over and over again. Reading for pleasure is how children learn to use good vocabulary, to recognize writing that works, and to create stories of their own.

All juvenile categories (Figure 24.2) are open to all readers entering the library. I have a habit of recommending children's titles I particularly enjoy to adults as well as to the children. I enjoy hearing the adult's comments when they return these titles. Nine times out of ten it was an enjoyable experience and they often ask for further recommendations.

It should also be noted here that the majority of public libraries allow children to borrow books from any area in the library. If you agree with this, say so in your borrowing policy!

Young Adult

Young adult (YA) fiction can be housed in its very own library area, or shelved in with the adult fiction. Young adult material often incorporates more adult concerns and topics (sexual awareness, heterosexual and homosexual relationships, self-esteem, suicide, parental discord, alcohol, drug use). I do not, therefore, shelve it with the juvenile novels. (I do not, however, discourage younger readers from borrowing these books. They will read what they can understand and more times than not they drift back into the children's section.) Shared shelving of adult and young adult, on the other hand, offers these subjects to young and all adults of all reading and interest levels.

IDENTIFYING

- If there's a separate young adult section, spine labels and catalogue cards will have a YA in the upper left corner. YA shows where it is shelved and what part of the collection this book belongs to.

- If you shelve the young adult fiction material with adult fiction, you may or may not need to put YA on the spine label,
- You do put YA on the shelf list card if you have a *separate* YA section because the shelf list cards reflect the exact shelf order of the library.
- If you have a combined fiction section, indicate on the catalogue card that it was purchased as YA material, in case you want to search for all YA titles.

SHELVING

Shelving order for fiction is the same as adult fiction (alphabetical), and any nonfiction you have expressly for young adults will follow the regular Dewey order. There are a few nonfiction subject areas that I think should be shelved within a separate young adult section if you have one. These include getting along with parents and siblings, beauty concerns, dating, self-esteem, peer pressure advice, and career considerations.

For the most part, though, young people of junior high and high school age will be using the adult nonfiction collection.

Circulation is discussed at the end of the chapter.

Adult Fiction

IDENTIFYING

If you shelve as one large section, you may want to identify genres of fiction. Genre spine labels allow your patrons to find the genre they like best on the shelf. These can be purchased from a library supplier or made by hand. Some examples are:

> Westerns = W, or horse symbol
> Mysteries = M, MYS, or sleuth with magnifying glass
> Short Story Collections = SS
> Science Fiction = SF or UFO symbol
> Fantasy = FAN, unicorn or wizard symbol.

This identification is something you may want to tackle after you have been open for a while—give yourselves a chance to see how the collection is used, and decide what is best for your patrons.

Right now, while you are just eager to get the books on the shelf, you can check the book's spine or cover for the author's name and shelve by that. Eventually, though, all adult fiction should have spine labels. In one alphabetized collection, each label would have FIC followed by the first three letters of the author's last name, and the same information will appear in the upper left corner of the circulation card. A full list of Adult Collection Spine Labels can be found on page 182 in Figure 24.5. Spine label identification accomplishes two things:

- It aids the staff in accurate reshelving, thus keeping the collection in good order.
- It aids patrons in finding authors they want.

SHELVING

There is a choice of how adult fiction can be shelved within its library area:

- Shelve all adult fiction together in one alphabetical order, using the authors' last name.
- Shelve the categories (or genres) of fiction each in its own section.

This choice applies to paperbacks as well as hard cover books.

When shelving adult fiction, I like to see some spaces showing throughout the shelving units. Use bookends to keep books neat and upright. Leave an open space every once in a while and stand a novel there with its jacket facing out. Book covers often tempt readers to try an author or a genre they have not tried before; it is a cheap way to advertise and circulate your collection. You may even discover, as I have done, a magic spot for displaying books: every book you place there is checked out! As you visit bookstores, you notice that they always have books on display, showing the artfully designed front covers. This is good marketing and good shelving!

Circulation of adult fiction is discussed at the end of the chapter.

Nonfiction Biographies

IDENTIFYING

Biographies are of course part of the nonfiction collection. For spine label identification we have the option of using:

- Dewey number 920
- The letters BIO
- Just the letter B.

Any are acceptable. Just be consistent. This identification will also be used on all cards.

Whichever of the three identification options you choose, you will shelve the books alphabetically by the *subject* of the book—and not by the author's last name. However, if it is an autobiography, the author and subject are the same. Thus, *Ben Holladay: The Stagecoach King* would be shelved by HOL (not FRE for J. V. Frederick, the author). A book about Abraham Lincoln would be shelved by LIN, not the author's name. A book about Nancy Reagan, by Nancy Reagan, would be shelved by REA for both subject and author.

All other nonfiction must be shelved first by its Dewey number. Within that same number group, next by the author's last name (first three initials) in alphabetical order.

Other Nonfiction

All nonfiction materials are arranged on the shelf by their "call number." This number belongs to a specific subject area. Classification systems arrange the subject areas and assign the call numbers. There are two classification systems most commonly used in libraries: Dewey Decimal System (Dewey), and Library of Congress (LC). Dewey uses numerals; LC uses letters and numerals.

The purpose of a classification system is to arrange together on the shelf all materials pertaining to a given subject. That is really all you have to know at this point.

Dewey is the system most used in public libraries, especially small ones. There is a natural flow to Dewey that you can experience if you have a chance to go to a large library and browse the shelves. You will notice how Earth Science, for example, begins at 500 with works on the whole general subject of the earth, and then travels through the 500s, into more specific parts and developments in the field of geology—volcanoes, glaciers and climate—then you are out into early life forms, up to dinosaurs, prehistoric man, and finally into mammals and Man. All the while, you will be in the 500s, with each narrower subject having its own number. A volunteer keen to try cataloguing found herself quite enthralled with this whole concept and enjoyed her volunteer hours immensely, while she was doing a wonderful service for the library!

The first piece of advice I can give on shelving nonfiction is:

Start grouping books together by general subject headings, using a good definition of each heading.

Use the summary of Dewey headings in Appendix A. Read it over until you are familiar with it and develop a feel for what goes where. I am giving the second level summary because it breaks down the very general headings such as Generalities, Law, Applied Science and Social Science into more familiar and useful headings. Ask your state library for further information about Dewey publications.

The second piece of advice is:

Carefully use the copyright page and Cataloguing-in-Publication (CIP) data.

This is almost always on the back of the title page in newer books; see what Dewey information the publisher gives you. Eighty percent of the time it is correct information, and at least it is a place to start. Continue to group books together within the subject headings they best fit. If you see a glaring difference, do the best you can.

Sample Nonfiction Spine Labels

Here are four imaginary nonfiction spine labels in incorrect order:

796 CUN	796 DOB	797 MON	796 MUN

Remember, arrange first by the number all the way through. Then within the books with the same exact number, by the alphabet. They should be:

796 CUN	796 DOB	796 MUN	797 MON

Another example incorrectly ordered:

636 BOT	636 FUL	636.1 HUN	636.1 HAN	636 LOB

The correct order should be:

636 BOT	636 FUL	636 LOB	636.1 HAN	636.1 HUN

Figure 24.5
SAMPLE SPINE LABELS FOR ADULT COLLECTION

CATEGORY OF BOOK	SPINE LABEL
Adult Fiction	FIC MOR
Westerns	W FIC L'AM
Science Fiction	SF FIC BRA
Mysteries	M FIC McB
Short Story Collections	SS FIC CHE
Biography	B (or 920) JEF (for Jefferson, not the author)
YOUNG ADULT Novels	YA FIC O'DE

YOUNG ADULT	YA
Nonfiction	123.4
	ABC
PAPERBACKS	Place under any of the above
For all of the above	PB (or LgPB)
Video	V-F
	M
Audio Book	AB
	FIC
(fiction)	MOR
Audio Book	AB
(nonfiction)	123.4
	ZIM
Reference	REF
	DIC
Reference	REF
(with Dewey)	413
	DIC-E

Circulating All Books

Refer to these sample book cards as we discuss the "how-to's" of circulation. I have shortened the length of the cards for spacing purposes.

```
FIC
CLA
PB
          Clancy, Tom
          Patriot Games

Patron #    Due Date
```

```
B
JEF
          Henry, Wallace
      Thomas Jefferson, Genius

Patron #    Due Date
```

```
YA
FIC
HIN
PB
            Hinton, S. E.
            The Outsiders


Patron #        Due Date
```

```
V-NF
W
            Wonders of the Earth


Patron #        Due Date
```

```
REF
423
DIC-F
LgPB
        French Dictionnaire


Patron #        Library Use Only
```

```
YA
746
SCH
LgPB
            Schrum, Harvey
        Decorating Your Own Room


Patron #        Due Date
```

You can see:

- All spine label information from chart is used in upper left corner
- A notation is needed; PB if paperback or LgPB if a large paperback (but *not* if it is hard cover) . *This applies to all categories.*

Once you have made cards:

- Place book cards in the book's pocket.
- Secure pocket inside the back cover of the book.
- These book cards stay filed at the library when the book goes out so you know which patron has the book.
- Use library stamp on at least three places in each book: on the lower edge inside front cover, inside back cover (on pocket), and once or twice on edges of book if thickness of book allows.

Note: I hate to deface books, even with library stamps, so I caution you against merrily stamping away over maps, portraits, family trees, diagrams and other important things placed inside either or both covers. You are just trying to identify the book as the library's—not cover it with stamping!

25

Cataloguing the Collection

Shelf List

When you begin collecting books for the shelf, you will want to maintain a record of which books you have. This record is called a shelf list and will ultimately reflect the exact shelf order of your collection. That is, there will be one card—or electronic entry—for each book exactly as it is found on a shelf within a particular area of the library.

Fiction books are shelved and shelf-listed in the alphabetical order of their author's last name. Nonfiction books are shelved and shelf-listed by their Dewey or Library of Congress number. Ideally, anyone should be able to take a shelf list and follow along the shelves, finding books in the same order as the cards.

This record enables libraries to take inventories and should be kept in a safe place, not available to patrons. In using a computer to record the shelf list, always copy it to a disc and store the disk where it will be safe from fire.

Figure 25.1 lists possible information which should go on the shelf list card:

Figure 25.1
SHELF-LIST CARD INFORMATION

Location	Author name—last, first, middle
Type	Title
Author	Responsibility
Format	Illustrator
	Publication info and date
	Series
	Note
	Number of pages
	Access points
ISBN	Subject headings
Price	Source

- *ISBN* number (ISBN) is the number assigned this, and only this, book. It is the International Standard Book Number, not a catalogue number. You can always identify a book by this number when ordering.
- *Price* is good to know if book has to be replaced (by patron or library).
- *Note* is a good place to mention what is special about this book—photos, maps, fold-outs, lists.
- *Access points* and *Subject headings* list all the ways this particular book can be found in the library catalogue (when it is completed.)
- *Source* in this case means where the book came from: vendor, gift, memorial.
- Location indicates where in library to locate book.
- Format indicates audio tape, video, large print, paperback, etc.

You may not need all these entries for every book; keep it as simple as you can. These terms will become clearer by looking at the following samples of both fiction and nonfiction. Use the samples that follow and Figure 25.1 as guides when you make your library's shelf list.

Shelf list card for a juvenile novel:

```
J FIC
FIE                             Field, Rachel
                                Hitty: Her first hundred years / Rachel Field
                                Illus.: Dorothy P/ Lathrop.
                                NY: The Macmillan Co. 1929


                                Note: 2nd printing of 1st Edition; color plates.
                                207 p.
ISBN        I title II. author 1. Dolls—New England—fiction.
$15.95 (current)   Donation.
```

Juvenile picture books:

```
J
S                               Sendak, Maurice
PB[paperback]
                                Where the wild things are / Maurice Sendak
                                NY : XYZ Co. 1965.


                                32 p.
                                I. title II. author


ISBN
$7.95                           Ingram
```

Adult fiction shelf list card for a novel:

```
FIC
HIL                             Hillerman, Tony
                                Fallen Man / Tony Hillerman.
                                New York: HarperCollins. 1996.


                                Series: Another Jim Chee novel

                                I. title II. author 1. Westerns—detective.
ISBN
$24.00  Smith Fund     Ingram.
```

For an adult paperback (format):

W [westerns]
L'AM
PB   L'Amour, Louis
                      The Sacketts: A Trilogy / Louis L'Amour
                      NY: Bantam. 1987.

ISBN   I. title. II. author. 1. Historical Fiction.
$5.95   Borders.

Nonfiction for hardcover, and then softcover books:

808.068 [put j after # if for juvenile]
COO
                              Cooper, Susan
                      Dreams and Wishes: essays on writing for children
                              / Susan Cooper.

                      New York : Margaret K . McEldery Books. 1996.

                      I. title II. author 1. Authorship. 2. Creative writing.
ISBN
$18.00   Gift from Kathleen Hamish.

```
W [Western Collection]
391
KOC
LgPB [large paperback]
                        Koch, Ronald P.
                        Dress Clothing of the Plains Indian /
                        Ronald P. Koch.
                        Norman, OK.: U. of Oklahoma Press. 1977.


                        Note: photos, techniques, comparison chart and
                        Bibliography.
                        219 p.
ISBN                    I. title II. author 1. Indians of North America—
Great Plains—Costume and adornment


$19.95                  U. of Oklahoma Press.
```

The shelf list card is the most important card to do. It should have all the information you will ever need on this book. If someone disagrees and decides to shorten the list, here are the items to include absolutely:

- *Type*—juvenile, fiction, nonfiction number; format; special collection location. This tells where the item is shelved.
- Complete *author name.*
- Complete *title.*
- All *publishing information and date* of the edition you have in your hand.
- *Format*—In the case of two versions of the same material, such as paperback or hardback. This identifies which version to replace, if needed.

Automated Catalogues

Even if you start with an automated catalogue system, you will need a hard copy of the shelf list for safekeeping. Computer systems have been known to erase everything in them, and if you lose this list, you will have to start all over!

Of course, computerized catalogue systems are a godsend to library staff! You need only to type in the above information, choosing which information you want included. You will not need to make all cards for the catalogue, although you will need to print one for the shelf list and one book card until you are completely automated and use bar codes with a scanner.

There is plenty of information out there on electronic systems. Some companies that are used by small libraries are:

> The Follett Software Corporation
> Telephone: 800-323-3397
> Internet address: http://www.fsc.follett.com/
> Winnebago Software Company
> Telephone: 800-533-5430
> Internet address: http://www.winnebago.com/index.htm
> Athena at Nichols Advanced Technology, Inc.
> Telephone: 800-642-4648
> Internet address: http://www.nichols.inc.com/products/athena.html

These three companies are widely used and have good reputations. They all have representatives eager to come and demonstrate their products to you. Please read about automated systems in general, before watching any dog and pony shows. System vendors will promise the stars, moon, and sun, and throw in the ocean to clinch the deal. That is their responsibility to the company they work for. Your responsibility is to get a system that will do what your library and community need. You may not need the stars, the moon *and* the sun.

Some things to consider:

• Can we start with just the catalogue?
• How easy is it to add the circulation system later on? Will we have to buy anything extra to compensate for the difference in the products' ages?
• How much patron information can we store and use?
• What kinds of confidential and security measures come with it?
• How much will it cost to have the company install the shelf list?
• Does it have full MaRC (Machine Readable Cataloguing—a method of standardized coding and cataloguing) record installed?
• How easy is it to switch from circulation to the catalogue?
• Do we get automatic upgrades, and how much are they?
• What kind of computer do we need? Can we use the one we have now?
• What free support can I expect right away and how much will continuing support cost?
• What kind of training is included with initial purchase? This is very important: with inadequate training, a system is wasted or used incorrectly.
• Are there libraries near enough so I can go and actually try a system?

There are some excellent books which will help you. Another good idea is to form a technology committee of people who are computer literate and can help narrow the choice of an automation system. This is not a one-person job!

— PART SIX —
GETTING MORE INFORMATION

26

Your State Library and State Library Association

Your State Library: Professional Collection, Directory of Libraries, Bulletins, State Library Associations

Every state has a state library; I advise you to get in touch with yours for several reasons.

- The state library should be an ally, not an adversary—it is just good politics.
- The state library will tell you if there is a county level system to which you automatically belong because of your geographical location. County systems can be as helpful, (if not more helpful) as the state level ones because they deal on a smaller, closer basis with "their" libraries.
- If there is no county level system, the state library can offer professional help to you via their staff.
- Libraries can become eligible for some financial help from the state library after meeting certain requirements particular to the state.

To be sure, some state libraries are more responsive to questions and requests than others, but it is always a good idea to give your state's library the benefit of the doubt and try to connect to it. If it becomes a great source of frustration and wasted time, you may want to "go it alone." This decision should be made, however, after you have investigated how much financial aid they can give you, and evaluated the requirements you must meet for that aid. Be that as it may, here are some simple ways you can benefit from the state library through their professional collection, directories, publications and associations.

PROFESSIONAL COLLECTION

Within the state library should be a professional collection: books written about libraries, librarianship, trusteeship, service, programming, and so forth. These are written for people in the field, and now that includes your group. Hopefully, your state library will have a list of titles to send you, then you can select the ones most helpful to your situation. Most state libraries will loan professional collection titles to libraries. This can be done by mail or in person. State library professional title lists may also have fax and telephone numbers of the publishers so you can purchase your own copies. I have included some of these in Chapter 29, Annotated Bibliography.

When you reach your state library:

- Ask for the person in charge of interlibrary loan of professional collection titles.
- Write down that contact person's name and extension.
- Be sure to ask how long the loan period is and exact address for returning the books.
- Ask if they include return postage labels. The United States Post Office offers a library rate for packages between two official libraries. As soon as you have your official name established at the Post Office, you can take advantage of the library rate. Until then, they offer a book rate to mail packages of books between a library and anyone else.
- Keep a list of what you request.

STATE DIRECTORY OF LIBRARIES

The state library should also be able to provide you with a directory of all libraries in the state, complete with addresses, telephone and fax numbers (e-mail addresses if they exist), personnel names, and the libraries' hours. There should also be a section on just the state library staff: the specific positions; what they cover; and who fills that position now, with telephone numbers included. If there is a charge for this state directory of libraries, it is worth the cost to have it on your shelf. The state library association may publish this directory instead of the state library, but ask anyway.

STATE LIBRARY BULLETIN,
OR SCHEDULE OF EVENTS

If the state library publishes a monthly or yearly schedule of events, ask to be put on their mailing list; these schedules will give you the places and times for helpful workshops. You may want to enter these dates on your planning calendar. Be sure to note any registration deadlines for what interests your group. Sometimes space is limited, and early registrants get the seats!

The State Library Association

State library associations are dedicated to supporting libraries in a variety of ways. They provide information on a regular basis (newsletters), they host annual or semiannual conferences and offer a forum for discussions. A listserv (an e-mail server) on the Internet may even be offered so librarians all over the state can talk to each other in an ongoing discussion. Within some states, there may be separate associations for school, public, and academic libraries. In many cases, however, they all belong to one Association.

There is usually a reasonable fee (or dues) for joining all associations. The fee may be set, or may be based on salary, expense budget or some other sliding scale mechanism. Individuals or a group may join.

I advise that initially one person join as a representative of your project right away to get all publications and registration news. As you continue, others may join or a library membership can be purchased. There is always someone in charge of membership in an association:

- Get their name from the state library.
- Call them to ask for a membership registration form.
- Ask to be sent the most recent past publication as soon as possible if the next one is not due out for some months.
- Keep person's name and telephone number.
- Keep a note of when you called and what you asked.

An association's newsletter or bulletin will give you an idea of what libraries around you are doing, when helpful workshops and conferences are scheduled, and you may even be able to post "classifieds" detailing what you need.

Interest Groups

Within the association there may be interest groups such as children's services, small public libraries, academic libraries, services to the handicapped and support staff. Your library or individual members can join any of these interest groups once they are members of the association. The groups may hold meetings around the state during the year, and they may host programs at conferences. Joining a group allows a chance to be with people from similar situations and interests; discussions and projects are specific to that interest.

Conferences

If you have ever been to a conference on anything at all, you know it can be exhilarating. It can also be exhausting, but if you're lucky, that exhaustion comes from trying to cram as much activity as possible into a short time frame!

Conferences usually consist of scheduled presentations, workshops, panel discussions and sometimes guest speakers, all having to do with a particular field. There are many wonderful opportunities to ask questions, actively take part in discussions and make new comrades-in-libraries. Most of all, you come away with a feeling that while you may have problems or dilemmas, others do too—you are not alone.

Board members, staff members, directors, state library staff, even retired librarians—all can be found at conferences, seeing old friends, keeping up with changes (trying to, at least!) and just generally recharging their library batteries. Schedules of events are sent out ahead of time so you can decide which program you want to go to in each time slot.

In the case of library associations, there should also be library product vendors set up with hands-on demonstrations, giveaways, examples of products, and lots of "good stuff" to see in person. It is much better to see some of these things than just to judge them from what you read. You can ask questions and pick up a myriad of catalogues, bookmarks, posters and business cards for future reference.

While there is a charge for registration at conferences (and you may need to stay overnight), finding a way to pay for this experience is worth the effort. Find someone who believes in the importance of libraries (and continuing education). Ask that person to sponsor a staff or board member to go to the conference. And give them nice recognition for doing so!

27

Our National Library
Association—ALA

The American Library Association, or ALA, is a giant organization in the national spotlight representing libraries of all kinds from all over the country. Headquartered in Chicago, ALA accepts memberships on a sliding scale determined by salary. For your membership, you receive reduced prices on all ALA publications, reduced registration at all conferences and a free subscription to their monthly publication *American Libraries*. You can also send for free information from any of their many divisions. They will send you a listing of all publications and divisions once you are a member.

An extension of ALA, the Round Tables, or special interest groups, represent various types of libraries and library core interests. I belong to PLA (Public Library Association.) You are automatically able to join one or more of these with ALA membership, and can also attend—at reduced rates—the conferences they host.

Joining ALA may be down the path for your group, but it is good to know it exists. The ALA represents libraries in all sorts of situations, both individually and collectively. It produces books and pamphlets on useful and informative subjects. It has an office in Washington, D.C., where it is continually watching for intellectual freedom infringement and other attempts at regulating dissemination of information. ALA is a real ally!

HOW TO REACH THE AMERICAN LIBRARY ASSOCIATION:

Mailing address:
   American Library Association
   50 East Huron Street
   Chicago, Illinois 60611
Telephone:
   800-545-2433
Fax:
   312-440-9374
Internet address:
   http://www.ala.org

28

Compatriots at Other Libraries

By deciding to create a library within your community, you have joined a whole network of people already engaged in library work. These people are now your compatriots. For the most part, they are willing and able to aid you in all aspects of the job you face. Other library personnel and board members can be wonderful sources of practical information.

Should you find one curmudgeon or disagreeable person, do not judge all library people by that experience. Move on to some other library or director, and find the answers that you seek!

Whether you live in a state profuse with libraries, or in one with very few, you can write to any library and ask for help. Letters can be addressed to the director or to the board of trustees.

Always be specific in your questions. Explain what you have already tried, or why you are having difficulty. When talking about the state library association, I suggested there may be a listserv on the Internet wherein you can pose these questions. You may get many responses from this source within a day or two.

When you travel, stop in libraries in the towns you pass through. You will get insight into signage, floor plan, and shelving. Let people know you're a library person, and most of the time, you will be engaged in conversation for quite a while! In my library, I am always delighted to have visitors so identify themselves—my staff and I have learned from these visitors' experiences, just as they have been interested in our efforts and successes.

Locally, try to meet with librarians to discuss issues and mutual concerns. If there is not a regional or district library arrangement, perhaps you can facilitate one. Libraries working together for the common good and reward of all concerned is not an unusual thing.

Ask to see library polices, long-range plans and other documents which will help you in formulating those of your own. If you can use the Internet, many libraries have these available on-line. It is not uncommon—as I have already said—to use someone else's policy or plan as a base from which to start constructing your own. Just make sure you tailor it to your community and abilities.

29

An Annotated
Bibliography

Since I have recommended you contact your state library for a list of their professional titles, I include here just a few titles I wish to call to your attention. They are not all brand new, but they all offer good advice and helpful suggestions. Though they are geared to library audiences familiar with library terminology and procedures, I think the volunteer library staff and board would still get useful information from any of them.

I suggest you create a list of titles (your own professional list) you find useful in any way, with notes as to particular usefulness. Often we want to find an explanation or reference and wish we could remember which book it was from. Also, there may be excellent examples of policies or procedures that you may need in a hurry.

The bibliographic entries here are listed by title first , then by author, publisher, year, and last by the Dewey Classification number (when available). Your state library may own all of them.

Developing Public Library Collections, Policies, and Procedures. Kay Ann Cassell and Elizabeth Futas. New York: Neal-Schuman, 1991. [DC 025.2187].
This book shows how small libraries can take information about their communities and use it to define and maintain the library's collection. The authors understand that low-budgeted libraries need all the help they can get.

The Dynamic Community Library: Creative, Practical, and Inexpensive Ideas for the Director. Beth Wheeler Fox. Chicago: American Library Association, 1988. [DC021.2].

> An excellent source, particularly Chapter 2: "The Ideal Library." It gives tips on analyzing the community, complete with sources of data, data collection, use of data, and community characteristics. The chapter goes on with suggestions for using this information in connection with library services such as programs, hours, special audiences, book selection and weeding, reference service, vertical files, literacy programs, and video and audio tapes. There is a checklist for library activities.

Great Ideas: The Library Awareness Handbook. Peggy Barber, editor. Chicago: American Library Association, 1982. [DC 021.7].

> Treating such areas as the end user, schools, newspapers, fund-raisers and special events, the author gives succinct examples of creating library awareness in every segment of the community. A good list of target audiences is given, along with how-to instructions.

Handbook for Small, Rural and Emerging Public Libraries. Anne Gervasi and Betty Kay Seibt. Phoenix, AZ: Oryx, 1988. [DC 027.4].

> This little paperback is stuffed with down-to-earth information, chapter by chapter. The sections are short and to the point. I think this is a good book to keep handy.

The Library Trustee. Fifth edition. Virginia G. Young. Chicago: American Library Association, 1995. [DC 021.82].

> This is a more studious work than the others, but gives an excellent view of trusteeship—its glories, joys and jobs. It is beautifully written and would benefit all library trustees.

Marketing the Library. Benedict A. Leetburger. White Plains, NY: Knowledge Industry Publications, 1982. [DC 021.7].

> Defining marketing as "a response to a need", the book covers techniques for programs, community relations and fund-raising. It gives examples of these—and more—and is encouraging in tone.

Planning for Automation: A How-to-Do-It Manual for Libraries. Second edition. John M. Cohn, Ann L. Kelsey, and Keith Michael Fiels. New York: Neal-Schuman, 1997. [na]

> A soup-to-nuts presentation, the authors provide the library technology team with the means to investigate, interview and chose a vendor for a new system. Suggestions for questions to ask, things to watch out for, and preparing a request for bid are just some of the useful things covered.

Small Libraries: A Handbook for Successful Management. Sally Gardner
Reed, Jefferson, NC: McFarland, 1991

    This book is written for "honest to goodness" small libraries, providing chapters
on collection development, facility enhancement, local government support, and
staff development.

Cataloguing Tools

    While these may seem steep in price, ultimately they are worth their
cost. Every library—no matter how small—that does cataloguing should have
at least two reliable and accurate tools to fall back on, even though most all
books now arrive with catalogue information on the copyright page.

Anglo-American Cataloguing Rules. Second Edition. Chicago: American
Library Association, 1998.

    For entering exact information into paper card catalogues and automated cata-
logue systems alike, this is an ultimate reference book.

    Take a look at one in another library, spend a little time with it and see why it is
so respected.

        ALA Order #3485-4-2054 (softcover)
        $55.00 (ALA members $49.50)
        ALA Order #3486-2-2054 (hardbound)
        $80.00 (ALA members $72.00) (1998 prices)

        Ordering Address:
        American Library Association
        ALA Editions
        50 East Huron Street
        Chicago, Illinois 60611-2795

Dewey Decimal Classification: A Practical Guide. Second edition. Lois Mai
Chan, et al. Revised for Dewey Decimal Classification 21. Albany, New York:
Forest Press, 1996.

    A guide for understanding and working with Dewey.

Dewey Decimal Classification and Relative Index. Melvil Dewey. Twenty-first
Edition. Volumes 1–4: Joan S. Mitchell, editor, Albany, New York: Forest
Press, 1996.

    In using Dewey, this book is what we all need when we do original cataloguing.
We learn how to identify which classification area to use for the book, and how to
build the Dewey number for it. Get this edition whenever possible: many changes
have been made to make Dewey compatible with today's language and usage.

Sears List of Subject Headings. Sixteenth Edition. Edited by Joseph Miller. New York: H. W. Wilson, 1997. ($54.00)

> Invaluable when struggling to decide which subject heading to use for a book! It has a superb introduction and guides you on how to choose the correct number and heading, while giving you more than one possibility. It will become a friend to all who use it! This is a good vehicle to use for double-checking classification information which the publisher has given to a book.

> *Ordering Address:*
> H. W. Wilson
> 950 University Avenue
> Bronx, New York 10452-4224
> Tel: 800-367-6770
> Fax: 800-590-1617

Subject Cataloging: A How-to-Do-It Workbook. Terry Ellen Ferl. New York: Neal-Schuman. 1991.

The OCLC (Online Computer Library Center, Inc.) is a nonprofit organization in Dublin, Ohio, devoted to library research and service. Memberships are offered.

> Telephone: 614-764-6000
> Internet addresses for OCLC Dewey tools:
> http://www.oclc.org/oclc/fp/index.htm
> http://www.oclc.org/oclc/fp/about/ddc21sm2.htm

Appendix

Dewey Decimal Classification 21: Summary 2

I choose to include Summary 2 because it divides the much more general Summary 1 into familiar categories of information. Within Summary 2, you will find useful numbers and can go from there to the *Sears List* for the more colloquial terms used by most patrons. Dewey defines the area and number; Sears translates those into subject headings, or access points.

000 Generalities
- 010 Bibliography
- 020 Library and Information Sciences
- 030 General Encyclopedic Works
- 040 [unassigned]
- 050 General Serial Publications
- 060 General Organizations and Museology
- 070 News Media, Journalism, Publishing
- 080 General Collections
- 090 Manuscripts and Rare Books

100 Philosophy and Psychology
- 110 Metaphysics
- 120 Epistemology—Causation, Humankind
- 130 Paranormal Phenomena
- 140 Specific Philosophical Schools
- 150 Psychology

160 Logic
170 Ethics (Moral Philosophy)
180 Ancient, Medieval, Oriental Philosophy
190 Modern Western Philosophy

200 Religion

210 Philosophy and Theory of Religion
220 Bible
230 Christianity and Christian Theology
240 Christian Moral and Devotional Theology
250 Christian Orders and Local Church
260 Social and Ecclesiastical Theology
270 History of Christianity and Christian Church
280 Christian Denominations and Sects
290 Comparative Religion and Other Religions

300 Social Sciences

310 Collections of General Statistics
320 Political Science
330 Economics
340 Law
350 Public Administration and Military Science
360 Social Problems and Services—Association
370 Education
380 Commerce, Communications, Transportation
390 Customs, Etiquette, Folklore

400 Language

410 Linguistics
420 English and Old English
430 Germanic Languages, German
440 Romance Languages, French
450 Italian, Romanian, Rhaeto-Romanic
460 Spanish and Portuguese Languages
470 Italic Languages, Latin
480 Hellenic Languages, Classical Greek
490 Other Languages

500 Natural Sciences and Mathematics

510 Mathematics
520 Astronomy and Allied Sciences
530 Physics
540 Chemistry and Allied Sciences
550 Earth Sciences
560 Paleontology, Paleozoology
570 Life Sciences, Biology

580 Plants
590 Animals

600 Technology (Applied Sciences)
610 Medical Sciences, Medicine
620 Engineering and Allied Operations
630 Agriculture and Related Technologies
640 Home Economics and Family Living
650 Management and Auxiliary Services
660 Chemical Engineering
670 Manufacturing
680 Manufacture for Specific Uses
690 Buildings

700 The Arts (Fine and Decorative Arts)
710 Civic and Landscape Art
720 Architecture
730 Plastic Arts and Sculpture
740 Drawing and Decorative Arts
750 Painting and Paintings
760 Graphic Arts, Printmaking and Prints
770 Photography and Photographs
780 Music
790 Recreational and Performing Arts

800 Literature and Rhetoric
810 American Literature in English
820 English and Old English Literature
830 Literatures of Germanic Languages
840 Literatures of Romance Languages
850 Italian, Romanian, Rhaeto-Romanic
860 Spanish and Portuguese Literatures
870 Italic Literatures, Latin
880 Hellenic Literatures, Classical Greek
890 Literatures of Other Languages

900 Geography and History
910 Geography and Travel
920 Biography, Genealogy, Insignia
930 History of Ancient World To Circa 499
940 General History of Europe
950 General History of Asia, Far East
960 General History of Africa
970 General History of North America
980 General History of South America
990 General History of Other Areas

OCLC (Online Computer Library Center, Inc.) was the source for Summary 2, and is located at http://www.oclc.org. Summary 3 (as you have probably guessed) further defines these areas. As you start shelving nonfiction, Summary 2 will get your books circulating; leave plenty of space on spine labels and cards for further numbering.

Make your own list of subject headings that occur in your collection. This should alert people as to what subjects you have so far included. What is not listed is not in your library "yet."

Though I included the Internet address for the OCLC's Dewey Decimal Classification and information in Chapter 29, I include it here also:

http://www.oclc.org/oclc/fp/index.htm
http://www.oclc.org/oclc/fp/about/ddc21sm2.htm

Another good on-line resource is the Library of Congress. There is a world of cataloguing information at the Library of Congress Internet address:

http://marvel.loc.gov/

Appendix

Chapter Worksheets

I like to work with tables, as you have noticed by now. If you have a computer and can design tables, that is great but not required.

1. Typed or hand-written lists are perfectly fine.
2. If you are typing or handwriting lists, make sure you have copies made of your finished products:
    - one for each core group member,
    - one for a permanent file.
3. Even if you save your work on a computer disc, every area covered in the worksheets should have an appropriately titled folder in the permanent file.

Basic tenet: Keep a record!

WORKSHEET 1.1
INTERESTS/EXPECTATIONS OF SUPPORTERS' GROUP

1. If these interest/expectations are shared in an open meeting, someone should serve as a recorder.

2. If a sign-up sheet is passed around, write "Passed" in the "Recorder" slot.

3. Make sure to date this sheet. If extra lists are made, date each one.

4. If you are not saving this on a computer, be sure to have at least three copies as insurance against loss.

5. Start an appropriately titled folder in the permanent file.

211

Date of Meeting: _____		Recorder: _____	
Interest/Expectation	*Name*	*Note/Experience*	*Phone, etc.*

WORSHEET 1.2
STATEMENT OF COMMITMENT

1. You may use the sample, but make sure to consider what the whole group considers basic to their commitment. There may be considerations particular to your group; no two are exactly the same.

2. If agreed, make sure everyone signs and that the paper is dated.

3. If you are not saving this on a computer, be sure to have at least three copies as insurance against loss.

4. Start an appropriately titled folder in the permanent file.

Statement Of Commitment
By The _____ Library Committee

We, the undersigned, do hereby pledge ourselves to the task of creating a library for _____. In doing so, we commit to the project by:

-
-
-
-
-

Signed: Date:
 1.
 2.
 3.
 4.
 5.

WORKSHEET 1.3
RECORD OF SEED MONEY FROM WITHIN CORE GROUP

1. Create a statement of why the group is committing this money.

2. Decide if you will take pledges or contributions only. Incorporate this decision into the statement.

3. Be sure to include plans for accounting of the money in the statement.

4. Design an attractive chart: Include names, amounts and dates. Remember—this will be what you show to future donors and others curious to see your intent.

5. You may opt to have individuals' handwritten signatures rather than a typed list of names.

6. If you are not saving this on a computer, be sure to have at least three copies as insurance against loss.

7. Start an appropriately titled folder in the permanent file.

WORKSHEET 1.4
POTENTIAL IN-KIND SERVICES RECORD

Decide how you want to set up your record of these services. Remember—these may be offered in lieu of cash contributions. Recordkeeping for these services is as important as monetary records. People like to know their offers are remembered and sought out when needed.

1. What are important things to record? Name of person, item or service offered, how do you get in touch with them when needed?

2. When would the service be available?

3. Would the person be interested in speaking to the core group about the service being offered?

4. Make sure you date the list.

5. Name of person who recorded the list if individuals aren't entering their own names.

6. If you are not saving this on a computer, be sure to have at least three copies as insurance against loss.

7. Start an appropriately titled folder in the permanent file.

Potential In-Kind Services
Date   Recorder

Person Offering	Service Offered	Phone	Dates Available

WORKSHEET 2.1
COMMUNITY CHARACTERISTICS

General Community Segments	How Our Community Reflects This Segment	Possible Representative from This Segment
Age Range		
Cultural Diversity		
Old-timers and Newcomers		
Education Establishments		
Business		
Service, Social and Religious Organizations		
Arts and Cultural Environment		
Local Government		
Other?		
Other?		

WORKSHEET 5.1
MISSION STATEMENT

1. Write down your library role(s).

2. List one or two goals the group would like to meet which are connected to that role.

3. Make a list of verbs which show intent to accomplish something.

4. Try a few verbs and then place the one you choose into a statement which begins: *Sample*: The Mission of the Handleberg Library Core Group (or Committee) is to or will (use your verb here) _____. And the statement then continues with your role and goal for that role.

5. Once you've crafted the mission statement, have all members sign and date the original, print out several copies. Frame the original!

WORKSHEET 5.2
CORE GROUP LOGO

1. Toss out ideas to each other of all things that are symbolic of a library and your community: books in different positions and shapes, computers, people reading, buildings, windows, trees of knowledge. Keep it simple. Could it be understood as being library related?

2. Sketch a familiar frame shape: diamond, circle, square, rectangle, oval.

3. Choose one or two ideas everyone likes and combine the symbol and the frame. Keep it simple!

4. If necessary, ask someone artistic to do a final sketch.

WORKSHEET 7.1
OBSERVATIONS

Try to look at a fact or group of facts and put in writing what you learned. If you used a list form for your facts, your population and school enrollment figures will probably act as the basis of your observations in almost every case.

EDUCATIONAL OBSERVATIONS

Our population is _____ and the total (all levels) school enrollment is _____. _____ % of the population is involved in some sort of educational pursuit. _____ of that figure have completed degrees of some level.

The (K–12) school enrollment is _____, and there are _____ in K–2 alone which is _____ % of the enrollment. That is a bigger percentage than other age groups. The superintendent's office says grade K has increased over the past three years. The total school enrollment will be increasing.

EMPLOYMENT & TRANSPORTATION OBSERVATIONS

Our population is _____, and _____ are employed. _____ % of those employed are self-employed, and are working at home. ___% work out of town or out of the county, and drive _____ minutes (hours) to work. They leave around _____ o'clock and return around _____. _____ people drive their own cars. _____ use public transportation. _____ people work in town, and _____ % of all employed in town walk to work.

These observations actually can be read aloud as a narrative. One sees the relationship between fact and observation. Try some on your own.

WORKSHEET 8.1
COMUNITY LIST

COMMUNITY LIST CONTENDERS:
How many can you name in your service area? List correct group name, contact person, telephone number and meeting times.

Governing Bodies: local & county
_____
_____

Churches
_____

Clubs: social, service, sport, other
_____
_____

Recreational Departments, Parks, or Programs
_____
_____

The Arts: writers, artists theaters, leagues, museums
_____
_____

Day Care Locations, all ages
_____

_____

Senior Citizen Facilities: residential or day care facilities
_____

_____

Health Facilities: hospitals or nursing homes
_____

_____

Communicators: editors and owners
_____

_____

Service Organizations: adult and juvenile
_____

_____

Low-income Housing Developments or Units
_____

_____

Schools: nursery, public, private, church, homeschool
_____

_____

Businesses & Professionals
_____

_____

Agencies: local, county, state
_____

_____

Special Interest Groups
_____

_____

Historical Societies & Town Historians
_____

_____

Agricultural Groups & Agencies: ranches, vineyards, orchards
_____

_____

Sports Groups
_____

_____

WORKSHEET 8.2
CONNECTIONS BETWEEN LIBRARY
AND THOSE ON THE COMMUNITY LIST

Write down connections that can be made between groups you want to reach and the groups (age, interest, locale) listed on the community list worksheet.

For each organizational information listed on Worksheet 8.1, add *ideas for cooperation and connections*. They should be mutually beneficial to both parties.

• Can the library do a program at an organization's meeting?
• Can a joint project be planned to benefit the whole community?
• Could an organization put up a display in the library?
• Could the organization meet at the library once a year?
• And so forth! Be creative.

WORKSHEET 9.1
LIBRARY SITE

Mark map of community with busy places: post office, food market, village or town hall, senior center, schools, Head Start building, bank(s), popular restaurant(s), gas stations, concentration of shops, and so forth.

WORKSHEET 9.2
LIBRARY SITE

(Prepare one for each potential site):

Site #1 _____

VISIBILITY

From how many directions can you see this location?

Does it face the street?

PARKING

Is there any parking area now?

How many cars can park easily? (Consider staff as well as patrons!)

Is there an adjacent or extra parking area close by?

Is it easy to get from parking area to building?

ACCESSIBILITY

Is the ground basically level for safe travel? (Consider elderly and young children.)

Is it now or can it be lit for safety in the evenings?

WORKSHEET 11.1
LIBRARY AREAS

1. List all the areas you would like to have in your library.

2. Decide how much space you have in the Library Building.

   • Can you combine areas? Give the rationale for doing so.

   • If you have a very large space you can have more than in a smaller space, but you still could combine some areas.

3. Prepare a statement about each area—defining it clearly so each area is unique as to what it contains.

WORKSHEET 12.1
FLOORPLAN

1. Review which library areas you selected. If you have not done so, read Chapter 11 on library areas now!

2. Cut out shapes for all library areas. These do not have to be straight lined! Use circles and let them overlap as you move them around—after all, that is what your areas will do, too.

3. Make a quick sketch of the floor area of your building and move the areas around until there is a good relationship between them.

WORKSHEET 13.1
EXTERIOR SIGNAGE

Remember: Placement, clarity, and consistency should guide you.

   • Make a list of all exterior signs you will want.
   • Find samples of lettering at the hardware or discount stores (stencils and wooden/plastic letters count, too!)
   • Hand write the words in different styles.
   • Cut cardboard to exact size of one sign you want. (Too big is better than too small.)

- Experiment with lettering samples you have.
- Experiment with borders—do they help or detract?
  Borders: wreaths, rope, simple frames, one line

When you've settled on a few ideas, go outside and try them where they will be placed. View them from several points to make sure their message is visible and clear. Check everything against the three principles!

WORKSHEET 13.2
INTERIOR SIGNAGE

1. Make a list of all the signs you will need in the library.
2. Divide them into the groups mentioned at the start of the Interior Signage section.
3. Assign a background color (paper) and letter style for each group.
4. Write up the above three steps as your Signage Policy.

Check everything against the three principles!

WORKSHEET 15.1
WISH LIST

Wish List for _____Library

The Library welcomes donations, but wishes them to be [condition, time of drop-off]

DONATION(S)

1. Clarification, details

2. Clarification, details

3. Clarification, details

[Statement about receipts (will be given in person only?)]

Signed by _____, Core Group   Date _____

WORKSHEET 15.2
DONATION POLICY

THINK ABOUT THESE QUESTIONS:

What do you want to make plain to donors or those interested in making donations?

What do you want to encourage?

What do you wish to avoid, if possible?

Will there be a receipt for donations? For all donations? For all monetary donations of ___ or more?

How will bulk donations of books be described? (I recommend "Four boxes of used books," or "one bag of used books," as opposed to spending the time to count each book. The donor can count if he or she wishes.)

Does the donor want books back that the library cannot use? How and when will the donor get them back from the Library?

If the donor does not want the books back, would the library want to sell them or give them to another source?

If there are other things that concern you about accepting donations, this is the place to cover those concerns and find a way to solve them.

Remember: A policy done before a crisis arises will keep confrontations and bad feelings from even beginning.

Index

223